HOME-COMING

A GUIDE TO GET _OUT OF YOUR HEAD_
AND _INTO YOUR HEART_

HOME-
COMING

Justine Harrington

"Owning our *story* can be hard but not nearly as difficult as spending our lives running from it. Embracing our vulnerabilities is risky but not nearly as dangerous as giving up on love and belonging and joy— the experiences that make us the most vulnerable. **Only when we are brave enough to explore the darkness will we discover the infinite power of our light.**"

—Brené Brown

Into Your Heart PRESS

HOMECOMING

A Guide to Get Out of Your Head and Into Your Heart

ISBN 978-1-5445-2039-1 (paperback)

To my mom, who held space for me
to find my heart.

Contents

1

What Is Healing?

INTRODUCTION

I'm going to be the girl who felt her feelings and died, I thought in between sobs and waves of uncontrollable grief.

I vaguely wondered if that would be a legitimate cause of death. It sure as hell felt like it in the moment.

I had made the decision to start feeling my feelings. The emotions that came up were so intense, so *heavy*, they felt never ending. I felt certain I would never feel another ounce of happiness again. In that moment, it seemed perfectly reasonable that I might die under the weight of my emotions.

I'm happy to report I didn't die. In fact, that was the beginning of me actually *living*.

Turns out, this was the start of my healing journey. As I began, I got to know myself in a deep and meaningful way. I learned to see myself with clarity and compassion. I learned to truly love myself.

I didn't know any of this when I made the decision to feel my feelings. All I knew was something had to give. I felt stuck. I was living in constant fear of failure and rejection. I felt undeserving of all the good people and things in my life. Deep down, I knew there had to be a different way to live.

I'd been going to therapy for years, and eventually I realized I never allowed myself to *feel*. I shoved my feelings down inside of myself or I numbed them in a variety of ways. The end result was a lifetime of bottled-up emotions weighing me down.

I knew I needed to start with my feelings so I could let go of the weight that was keeping me feeling stuck and living in fear.

I made the decision to feel the feelings I'd bottled up for most of my life, which is something I will also teach you to do.

I journaled about past experiences, I focused on what my emotions felt like in my body, and I worked toward giving myself permission to feel.

My old bottled-up emotions started to bubble up to the surface on my thirtieth birthday, which in my book will be forever known as ***The Day I Started to Feel My Feelings***.

I woke up to my husband cooking a big birthday breakfast for me. When I sat down at the kitchen counter to eat, I suddenly felt a huge and uncontrollable wave of sadness wash over me. I started to cry. I didn't just tear up and sniffle. I ugly cried. I felt overwhelmingly sad and lonely, despite the fact that my husband was standing in front of me with a plate full of sizzling bacon and eggs.

I ran from the room in tears and plopped on my bed. I refused to speak to anyone, and I spent most of the day crying and feeling tsunami waves of sadness, despair, and loneliness.

Eventually, as any scared thirty-year-old experiencing her feelings for the first time would do, I called my mom.

Through tears, I asked her, "When is this going to end?"

For most of my life, I wasn't aware.

I wasn't aware that my actions and behaviors were driven by fear.

I wasn't aware that my wounded words and actions hurt the people around me.

I wasn't aware of all the ways I was hurting myself.

I wasn't aware of my conditioned behaviors, thoughts, and beliefs—the behaviors, thoughts, and beliefs I picked up from others or learned through my experiences.

I wasn't aware that these behaviors, thoughts, and beliefs were learned, and that I could also unlearn them and replace them with thoughts and beliefs that served me.

I became aware because others on their own healing journeys shared their stories and experiences with me. They showed me a path of self-exploration and compassion that I didn't know existed.

My intention for this workbook is to do the same for you. I want to show you there are many paths available to you.

You do not have to continue to feel less than, unworthy, or fearful. You can build a new reality for yourself.

If you feel stuck, limited, or stunted in your growth.

If you obsess over what other people think of you.

If you feel like you need to prove you belong.

If you are constantly people-pleasing at the detriment of your own happiness or needs.

If you are terrified to enjoy the good things in your life because you're afraid they'll disappear.

If you think everyone else has life figured out and you're just treading water, trying to stay afloat.

If you see unhealthy patterns playing out in your life that you want to stop, but you don't know how.

If you know the person you want to become, but have no idea how to get there.

This workbook is for you.

I offer tools and practices to help you understand yourself, see yourself with more clarity, connect with your body and your emotions, and ultimately live from a place of love rather than fear.

I've created this workbook because I've embarked on my own healing journey *and* I'm an analytical, process-oriented thinker. I felt called to break down the exact steps I took in my journey to better understand the process and to share it with others.

As you walk through the process I've outlined and embark on your journey, please know there is no finish line.

There is no checkbox that's labeled, "I'm healed!" (Wouldn't that be nice, though?)

As a list-lover who delights in that small hit of dopamine when I check something off my to-do list, this is something I struggle with. I want a freaking checkbox I can check off as a sign of accomplishment!

The goal, and the accomplishment, is more subtle.

Once you begin to heal yourself, you uncover a new way of living—a new way of being.

You will naturally begin to feel ease where you once felt tension.

You will feel a sense of freedom from your own expectations and judgments.

You will feel a sense of peace within that comes with deeply knowing yourself.

You will love all parts of yourself, even the parts you might be scared to look at right now.

You will sink into the beautiful and loving you that has always been underneath the conditioned layers you've accumulated throughout your life.

The more layers you peel back, the more layers you will realize are hidden underneath. You will most likely have the same epiphany several times, each time with a different perspective. From my experience, each time you will feel more compassion and empathy toward yourself and others.

This is the accomplishment—a new way of being based on compassion, empathy, love, and freedom.

The expectation is *not* that you will be healed at the end of reading through this workbook, but rather that you will gain actionable tools to guide you within yourself. You will have tools you can use over and over again as you walk your own path of healing, wherever that path may lead you.

WHAT IS HEALING?

I recently asked a group of close friends, "What does healing mean to you?"

My wise and dear friend, Brittany, described healing as a homecoming, a return to self. She described it as the process of stripping away all the conditioned thoughts and beliefs that are not ours. Repeatedly seeking to tell ourselves the truth about our own behaviors, thoughts, emotions, beliefs, and experiences.

I love this definition, and it deeply resonates with my own experience. What healing means to you might be different than what it means to me. I believe it's a concept that continues to evolve along with our own growth and evolution.

In this workbook, I explore what healing has meant to me over the years of developing my own connection to self. My definition and conceptualization of healing is in no way exhaustive, but simply a reflection of my journey and current understanding.

For me, healing is cultivating the practice of Going Within.

Healing happens *within* us. Healing does not happen externally. It is not creating a new self-care routine, starting yoga, or drinking green juice.

Don't get me wrong. All these things are great, but healing isn't what you do—it goes much deeper than that.

Healing happens within your mind and body. Healing is finding your true sense of self within and celebrating your wholeness, rather than looking at where you are lacking.

Healing is knowing yourself fully and deeply. It means accepting all parts of yourself, *especially* the parts you might currently think of as "less than."

To deeply heal yourself and live from a place of love, you *must* Go Within.

WHAT DOES IT MEAN TO GO WITHIN?

Our minds and bodies store all of the memories, experiences, emotions, and programming that make us who we are. We need to intentionally connect with and explore our minds and bodies to more fully understand ourselves.

Our conscious mind is the steady stream of thoughts running through our head, but the majority of our mind is below our everyday conscious awareness, in our subconscious.

Our subconscious mind stores everything that makes us who we are—our past experiences, memories, and beliefs, and these deeply influence our behaviors, thoughts, actions, and decisions.

The elusive yet influential subconscious feeds information to our conscious awareness. Basically, it is running the show, which is why it's important to learn to tap into your subconscious to understand the forces influencing your behaviors and thoughts.

Emotions are energies. If they are healthily processed, they move through the body and are released.

When an emotion is too overwhelming, the body goes into *freeze* response, and the energy gets stuck. It's then stored in the surrounding tissue.

Because of this, emotions, memories, and traumas from throughout our lives can be stored in our bodies if they were not properly processed in the moment of an emotional or traumatic experience.

Unprocessed emotions can have negative implications, which include mental and physical disease.

Common neck and back pain can be caused by syndromes such as Tension Myoneural Syndrome (TMS), which is physical pain caused by repressed emotions.

Research indicates the pain of TMS is the mind's defense to prevent repressed emotions from becoming conscious. Essentially, the physical pain is a distraction to keep painful emotions buried. Even more shocking is that around 80 percent of the population has experienced pain from TMS.[1]

Furthermore, research has shown that over 80 percent of all physicians' visits have to do with a socioemotional challenge, while only 16 percent could be considered solely pathophysiologic in nature.[2] In other words, unfelt emotions cause people physical pain and contribute to a number of medical issues.

From the subconscious mind all the way to the information stored in our bodies, there's *a lot* going on underneath the surface of the mind that influences who we are, how we feel, how we act, our everyday decisions, how we treat ourselves and others, and our relationships.

If we don't dig deeper into our minds and connect with our bodies, we remain a passenger throughout the journey of our life.

We are not fully aware of who's driving.

We are not in control of the destination.

---

1 John E. Sarno, MD, Healing Back Pain: the Mind-Body Connection (New York: Grand Central Publishing, 2018).

2 International Journal of Psychotherapy Practice and Research, Pen Access Pub, accessed February 22, 2021, https://openaccesspub.org/ijpr/article/999.

We are just along for the ride.

THE GOING WITHIN PROCESS

I created The Going Within Process as a step-by-step guide to help others dive into these deeper parts of themselves—to peel back their layers and begin to understand the conscious and unconscious influencers that drive their behaviors.

The process guides you to question your behaviors, thoughts, and emotions as a way to tap into your subconscious mind and connect with the physical sensations and messages from your body.

By connecting with your subconscious mind and your body, you begin to more deeply know yourself. You begin to understand when your behaviors and thoughts are coming from a wounded place inside of you, rather than a place of wholeness and love.

With this connection to yourself and increased clarity, you can begin to intentionally build beliefs and behaviors that serve you, rather than blindly reacting based on buried emotions and outdated beliefs.

The Going Within Process guides you from the behavior you are seeking to change to the belief that your behavior is rooted in. Through the process, you will gain a deeper understanding of yourself and how to create lasting, impactful change in your life.

The final section of this workbook walks you through The Going Within Process. I share my own experience, then offer you guidance and writing exercises for you to explore each layer of yourself with the intention of dismantling outdated beliefs and building new ones that serve your greatest good.

Before you Go Within, you'll first learn the tools needed to support the process.

In the second section of this workbook, you'll learn to face the uncomfortable parts of yourself, observe your thoughts, identify, and stop The Fear Spiral of Doom, feel your feelings, connect with your needs, and see the magic and beauty within yourself.

These are all tools I learned along my journey that have deeply impacted my life and continue to support me to this day. I share them with you so they can also support you as you Go Within.

I invite you to work through the following chapters slowly and intentionally.

Take your time learning the tools.

Take breaks as needed.

And always remember why you started this journey in the first place.

CHAPTER 1

My Breaking Points

MY FIRST BREAKING POINT (oh yes, there's more than one!) came a couple of months after I started working at Scribe Media, the amazing company who helped me publish this book!

Scribe Media holds an annual Summit where the entire company gathers for a week of learning, connecting, and bonding.

I was in the "hot seat" of an activity we call Strengths & Obstacles (affectionately, S&O for short).

Everyone gathers around one person and showers them with love by pointing out their strengths and areas where they kick ass. Then, that person shares the goals they're working toward, and everyone helps them identify any obstacles standing in the way of achieving those goals.

One of the co-founders leads the exercise. He is what I call a mirror of truth, meaning he will reflect *exactly* what you need to hear, even if it's a tough truth.

That is the beauty of the S&O exercise. You are told exactly what you need to hear by people who love, care for, and support you.

Oftentimes, exactly what you need to hear *is* a tough truth: something you're blind to in the moment, but others can see crystal clear from the outside. Because of this, S&O can be emotional and at times even contentious, but it is ultimately a rewarding and profound experience.

For me, being in the hot seat was nerve-racking as hell. I cringed at the thought of being the center of attention and having so many eyes on me. It made the hot seat feel *especially* hot.

After being showered with love as others excitedly shared the strengths they saw in me that I couldn't see for myself, it was time for revealing my goals...and what was keeping me from achieving them.

I squirmed a bit as I shared my goal to grow into a leadership position at the company.

The feedback was unanimous. First, I needed to connect with myself and my emotions before I could ever truly empathize with others and become an effective leader of people.

I accepted the feedback and the conversation quickly moved on, but the words didn't really sink in. Honestly, I wasn't sure what it meant to connect with my emotions. I was in a happy relationship, I had great friends, and I loved working at Scribe. Everything in my life seemed fine. What else did I need to connect with?

Turns out I had a whole lot of emotions and experiences underneath the surface to connect with, but we'll get more into that later.

Afterward, I sat on the fluffy green lawn of the Colorado cabin where Summit was held that year, chatting with a coworker. I mentioned that my S&O felt easier than others I had witnessed. There were no hard truths, no tears, no contention. It was just *easy*.

"You are not ready for that," my coworker responded. "You have really high walls up. You don't let others in easily. We don't want to push you too hard."

Now **THIS** sunk in. I have walls up!? I don't let others in? I worried that I seemed weak, like I would break if I was pushed too hard.

This seems like a problem, I thought, and I promptly made up my mind to fix the problem.

When I returned home from Summit, a couple of things happened in quick succession. First, I made an appointment with a therapist I would continue to see for a couple of years. Next, in typical Justine fashion, I uprooted my life to "start again."

After a not-so-good track record of unhealthy relationships, I was finally in a loving relationship based on mutual respect and trust. But, I believed I needed to be by myself to connect with myself, so I broke up with my then-boyfriend (now husband), moved out of our condo, and almost forcefully began to explore who I was behind the walls.

I felt uncomfortable in therapy at first. Everything was about *me*. She asked me where I wanted to begin each session. (I wanted to respond, "I don't know. Where do *you* want to begin?") She gently pushed to know more about me. She asked questions to steer the conversation back to my feelings and perspective.

This was the first time I had ever allowed a whole hour dedicated wholly to me, my needs, my emotions, my struggles. Initially the spotlight on me felt bright and awkward, but I slowly began to feel more comfortable. I connected with myself and led the conversation.

Through working with my therapist, I began to acknowledge my limiting behavior patterns. These were the behaviors that I didn't like about myself that were limiting my growth and connection with myself and others.

These behaviors were "The Wall."

My pattern was to keep people at a distance. I self-sabotaged my way out of situations and relationships that made me feel *less than*. I opted out and knocked myself down a notch along the way before ever opening myself up to being vulnerable to others. I created the hurt before someone else could. (Hence the sudden breakup with my boyfriend, who was as caring and supportive as they come.)

I had difficulty letting others in because my mind was always swirling with doubt and uncertainty around what other people thought of me. I constantly ruminated about how others perceived me. My mind was my own worst enemy, often tricking me into believing the worst about myself.

I stayed disconnected from myself because it seemed easier than examining the overwhelmingly critical thoughts that reeled through my mind on a daily basis.

To change my limiting behavior and thought patterns, I needed to do just that. For the first time in my adult life, I sought to see myself truthfully and objectively.

Along with my therapist, I worked to acknowledge and accept all parts of myself, *especially* the parts I wanted to hide from.

This meant acknowledging the pain that I previously ignored, looking at the deep pockets of fear and shame within myself, and seeing all the ways I was hurting myself and others.

The process of seeing myself clearly, including the ways I had been limiting myself and (maybe not so) subtly keeping myself small and afraid was challenging and painful.

But in this process, I learned so much about myself. I healed parts of myself and I healed relationships that needed mending. I began to recognize my own strengths, and I learned how to show up for myself and others.

Fast forward three years, and I'm in the S&O hot seat again.

I had come a long way in my personal growth since the last time I was in the hot seat, but as I sat there with my newfound perspectives and self-awareness, I felt like an imposter.

I looked at all the faces circled around me. I admired and cared for these people. I also felt undeserving of the kind things they said about me.

I wanted so badly to be open and receptive to their love. I reminded myself to let their caring and loving words sink in, but I couldn't fully accept them.

Here, in the hot seat yet again, I reached my second breaking point. (Coincidence? Probably not.)

On a logical level, I *knew* I was surrounded by people who loved me, but I couldn't for the life of me open myself up to *feel* loved.

The same was true for all my relationships. I had gotten back together with my boyfriend a couple of months after the initial breakup. By the time I reached this second hot seat breaking point, we had been married almost a year. Our relationship was better than ever, yet I still felt a twinge of unworthiness—like I didn't deserve that much happiness.

I sat in the hot seat, desperately trying to feel the love that surrounded me, when it hit me. The fear, shame, and insecurity I had worked HARD to acknowledge over the past three years were **still** influencing my sense of self. I still felt a sense of unworthiness that affected my life and relationships with others.

I had stopped my blatantly destructive behavior patterns by acknowledging past traumas and the fear and shame that were alive in me because of them.

But, in many areas of my life, these feelings were still subtly running the show. The destruction was less obvious, but still very present.

In that moment, I uncovered a deeply important self-truth: acknowledging my emotions of fear and shame were not the same as actually *feeling* these feelings.

Whoop, there it is.

I had tricked myself into believing that mentally acknowledging my feelings was the same as actually feeling them.

This illusion came crashing down that day in the hot seat when I painfully realized the difference between knowing that someone loves me and actually feeling the sensation of *being loved*.

After this realization, I consciously and intentionally worked toward feeling my feelings.

I began to pause throughout my day with the intention of giving myself space to feel. Through this process, I acknowledged my instinct when heavy emotions came up. I wanted to *do something*. I wanted to have a glass of wine, pick up my phone and scroll through Instagram, finish a work task, run an errand...*anything* to stay busy and not feel.

I had learned and grown with my first therapist, but at this point, I felt it was time to move on. I searched for a new therapist with the intention of finding someone who could help me connect with my emotions.

As I slowly opened myself up to my feelings, I started to uncover and feel waves of old, intense emotions associated with past experiences. I quickly learned the feelings I had shoved down deep inside didn't simply disappear.

My mind had created elaborate stories to distance myself from my painful emotions, but these unfelt feelings dug deep into me and became woven into the fabric of my being.

The weighty emotions that seemed too overwhelming and scary to feel became part of who I was and negatively influenced my behavior and thought patterns.

Feeling scared of or overwhelmed by intense emotions is totally normal. If you aren't scared, you're probably not being honest with yourself.

Feelings like grief and fear have a weight of permanence. They feel never ending.

Just like the first wave of intense emotions I uncovered on my thirtieth birthday, there have been times I believed I'd be crushed under the weight of my emotions.

Despite what they feel like in the moment, feelings can't crush or kill you. Feelings ebb and flow and are anything but permanent. But in moments of grief and despair, the overwhelm and sensation of permanence is potent.

When I began my practice of Going Within and worked toward feeling the emotions I'd been hiding from, which you'll learn to do throughout this workbook, I totally understood why I'd avoided them my whole life.

They're overwhelming!

They're uncomfortable!

They're inconvenient!

They're painful!

But, they're also temporary.

Once an emotion is fully felt and expressed, it's gone.

There's also the flip side to feeling your feelings, which is what brought me down the path of feeling in the first place.

As I began to uncover and feel my feelings, I noticed a new lightness. I laughed more often and more deeply. I felt a new depth of connection and openness toward love. I felt more playful and more open to joy.

With this new lightness, I was reassured of my reasoning for working toward feeling my feelings. By distancing myself from my weighty emotions, I also distanced myself from feeling the lightness and playfulness of love and joy.

I had been stuck in the middle lane, never veering too far from my comfortable numbness.

TAKING THE FIRST STEP
ON YOUR HEALING JOURNEY

Maybe you've had your own breaking point that led you here, to this workbook. Maybe you're ahead of the curve and avoiding your breaking point altogether. Either way, you've already taken the first steps on your healing journey.

Healing means getting to know your true self—the you beneath the behaviors, thoughts, and beliefs you picked up from others or learned through your experiences.

Many of your learned behaviors, thoughts, and beliefs were learned early in life as a way to understand the world and how to meet your needs in order to survive.

Early in life we are dependent on others for survival, and we perceive the world and our experiences through the primitive lens of our survival instincts. When we're children, being loved and cared for means we are safe.

As children, we interpret feelings of love as safety and feelings of loneliness as unsafe. And for a good reason too. Research shows that feelings of loneliness as an infant are actually a matter of life and death. Babies can die of loneliness, even if their other basic needs are met.[3]

Our early learned beliefs and behaviors can grow from a place of fear, and in our adult lives they may continue to limit us and keep us playing and feeling small. Or even worse, they could be downright toxic and harmful to ourselves and to others.

We are so much more than our conditioned behaviors, thought patterns, and beliefs, and the healing journey helps us to truly see all of ourselves.

Only when we truly see ourselves—including our own conditioning and learned ways of being—can we *unconditionally* love ourselves.

---

3 Harry Bakwin, MD, "Loneliness in Infants," American Journal of Diseases of Children, JAMA Network (January 1, 1942), https://jamanetwork.com/journals/jamapediatrics/article-abstract/1179366.

As psychologist and psychoanalyst Alice Miller writes in her book *The Drama of the Gifted Child*, "We can repair ourselves and gain our lost integrity by choosing to look more closely at the knowledge that is stored inside our bodies and bringing this knowledge closer to our awareness...We become free by transforming ourselves from unaware victims of the past into responsible individuals in the present, who are aware of our past and are thus able to live with it."

When I first started my healing journey, I was scared to look within and find out who I really was. At the time, I wasn't fully aware of the extent I had been hiding from myself (and others), but I was aware of a deep fear that I was intrinsically "bad." I was fearful I would find a monster within.

Looking within was the very thing that saved me from my own suffering, but it was also the thing I was most terrified of.

I suspect this is true for many of us, especially as we start our healing journey. We've become accustomed to being closed off and disconnected from ourselves, and it can feel scary and overwhelming to shed light on the darkness.

When I was young, around eight years old, I was terrified there were monsters in my closet. The darkness of night exacerbated my fear, and I could have sworn I saw things creep and crawl in my room during the night. I would scream for my mom, who came and turned on my bedroom light to expose there was nothing at all creepy, crawly, or scary in my room. My mind was playing tricks on me.

Our minds never stop playing tricks on us. The mind creates its own version of reality based on past experiences and the need to protect ourselves. We're wired for survival, and the brain does not know the difference between emotional pain and physical pain—it wants to avoid it all.

The fear of unseen monsters lurking in my closet is the same fear I felt about Going Within myself to find out who I really am. I was terrified I would find a monster when I switched on the light to expose the darkness within.

Just like when I was eight years old, the light forced me to realize the monsters were all in my head. They were not real.

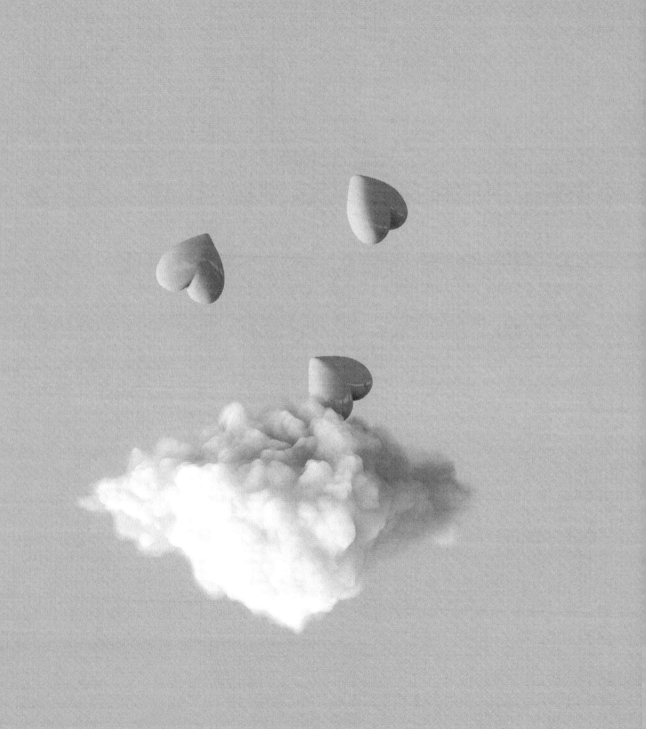

Explore and Connect with Yourself

CHAPTER 2

The Shame Game

SHAME IS THE FIRST CHAPTER in this section because I believe talking about and helping to normalize shame is one of the most important things I can do.

This is also the very last chapter I wrote. As much as I believe in the importance of sharing my story and talking about shame, it is not easy.

When I first started to explore the shame I held within, I made a bullet-point list of my past experiences and actions that I felt ashamed of.

The list was LONG, and writing it out was NOT FUN.

I then read the entire list out loud to my therapist. My voice cracked the entire time. I took long pauses to muster up the courage to speak some of the things out loud. I cried. I didn't look up even once from the piece of paper I held in my hands.

When I got to the end of the list, I braced myself and thought, *Okay, this is when I look up and see her horrified face.*

I was convinced she was judging me as she silently crafted her escape plan for how to fire me as a client.

When I looked up from my bulleted list, I saw that her face wasn't at all horri-fied. If I could sum up her facial expression in one word, it was pure empathy.

She told me I was courageous.

We talked about how the experiences I shared happened when I was young and in survival mode.

She reminded me that as a teenager, I didn't have the emotional intelligence or tools that I have now, and it was a disservice to me to hold my past self to my current standards.

Our discussion was helpful, but the most impactful part of that experience was receiving compassion and empathy when I expected to receive judgment and ridicule.

Why did I expect to receive judgment and ridicule? Because I had been judging and ridiculing myself about these things my entire life.

Shame is a very real, powerful emotion, but its power comes from our unwilling-ness to look at, feel, and share our shame. Like the monsters in my closet as a kid, shame thrives in the darkness, and once we bring it to light, we see it's not at all what we were expecting.

When we bring our shame to light, it no longer holds power over our beliefs, our thoughts, our fears.

Shame no longer controls us.

· ♥ ·

Society piles shame onto us from a young age. We're taught gender norms, and both boys and girls are taught to suppress parts of themselves to fit into the norm. Boys learn to feel shame around their emotions; girls learn to feel shame around their voice and assertiveness.

My intention is not to get into all the ways in which society shames us. This is meant to be a basic example of how shame is woven into the fabric of our upbringing. You don't need to have specific events that you regret or feel shame around (although all of us do). Simply being a human on this planet means you have felt or hold shame within yourself.

Shame is a universal human emotion. We have all felt (or, let's be real, tried not to feel) shame, but we don't want to acknowledge it because shame is painful and makes us feel less than.

You may not yet have acknowledged your own feelings or beliefs around shame, and that is okay. Shame is a powerful and complex emotion that is intricately woven into the human experience in ways we often don't even realize.

In other words, shame is so common and so human that it naturally becomes part of who we are without us even realizing it's there.

If you're reading this workbook, you're likely curious about yourself, even when it comes to the uncomfortable parts, like shame. The exercise at the end of this chapter will help you begin to explore what shame means to you at this point in time, and it is a resource you can return to as many times as you need to.

Just know: whether you currently feel overwhelmed with shame, or if you think you're the one true exemption to shame, I have been where you are. I have been blind to my shame, and I have been overwhelmed by my shame—these are both normal parts of the process.

If there was one thing that would have stopped me from taking the first steps in my healing journey, it would have been my own shame, which is why it's so important to bring this to the surface and acknowledge this complex emotion. When we don't acknowledge our shame, the weight of it keeps us from reaching our greatest potential.

Throughout my twenties, I felt deep shame around "the person I used to be." With every year that passed, I had another year of experiences to add to my shame list, but a lot of my shame was centered around my teenage years.

When I was fourteen, my mom came out as gay, divorced my dad, and moved away. I felt deeply abandoned and hurt in ways I couldn't even begin to understand at the time. The trauma of feeling abandoned by my mom triggered a domino effect of toxic behaviors and poor decisions that cascaded beyond my teenage years.

As a teenager, I took my pain out in a lot of harmful ways to myself, and I was hurtful to the people around me. I binge-drank, partied, got into fights, was arrested more than once, and generally wasn't a nice person.

Throughout my twenties, I hated that teenage version of myself, and this hate was deeply rooted in shame. Shame defined me, kept me rooted in a place of hate—very far away from loving myself—and kept me feeling small and fearful.

Researcher and author Brené Brown says, "Shame is the most powerful, master emotion. It's the fear that we're not good enough."

I held onto and ignored so much shame that I deeply internalized this fear and believed I wasn't good enough—not good enough to be loved and accepted by others.

I see this now, after beginning to peel back my layers of shame and associated beliefs. At the time, though, I had no idea how much shame I held inside, and I could not even begin to see how shame ultimately controlled my inner world and sense of self.

Shame is a restricting emotion that closes you off from yourself and, as a result, closes you off from others. Shame keeps you from the connection with self and others we all innately crave as humans.

I know this because this was my own experience.

Shame built and maintained a wall around my heart.

Shame kept me from fully and deeply knowing myself, and therefore kept me from fully and deeply loving myself.

Shame is one of the most manipulative, deceitful, toxic emotions because the very nature of shame keeps us in a fearful state of nonliving.

A unique characteristic of shame is that it generally breeds more shame. I was ashamed of my shame, so I shoved it down inside and tried to ignore it.

By not acknowledging my shame, it continued to build and build and build within me.

I became more and more disconnected from and afraid of myself.

The wall around my heart grew bigger and stronger.

I built a fortress of shame around my heart and wouldn't even let myself inside.

Can you imagine living with a Shame Fortress inside of you?

The Shame Fortress is far more painful than looking at and feeling the actual shame.

Suffering is the resistance of pain. We cause our own suffering by resisting the emotions we don't want to feel. This concept is a teaching of Buddhism that continues to be expanded on by modern psychologists and meditation practitioners.

We all have the choice to face whatever is within us that we don't want to look at. When we continue to ignore and repress it, we cause our own suffering.

When we choose to look at and feel our painful emotions, it is uncomfortable and, well, painful, but these feelings are temporary. Suffering is eternal until we make the choice to let go of the resistance and Go Within.

Another profoundly impactful experience with sharing my shame was when I wrote and delivered my One Last Talk to a small group of people at a writing workshop.

The premise of One Last Talk is to write and share your truth by answering the question: If you were about to leave this planet, what would you say, and who would you say it to? (The *One Last Talk* book guides you through a step-by-step process for doing this and is listed in the Resources section at the end of this book.)

For me and many others who have written their One Last Talk, writing and sharing my truth meant writing about the parts of my past I felt the most shame about.

When I sat down to write my One Last Talk, I knew exactly what I needed to write. About a year after writing out my initial shame list to share with my therapist, new layers and levels of understanding about my own story had emerged. My One Last Talk went much deeper into my emotions, behaviors, and thought patterns than the original list.

My One Last Talk was surprisingly easy to write, but as soon as the words were in black and white on the screen, my mind freaked out. I literally had to go for a walk around the block in thirty-degree January weather to calm down and keep myself from deleting everything I had just written.

My mind was screaming at me, *You can't share this with other people! They'll judge you, they'll be disgusted by you, they'll reject you!*

I couldn't even bring myself to save the document on my computer out of fear someone might hack into my computer, find the document, and widespread share it on the internet. The odds of that actually happening are basically zero, but in the moment this was my literal, albeit irrational, fear.

I printed out two copies of my talk and closed out the Word doc, clicking "Do not save" on the way.

My whole body was shaking when I delivered my talk in a small room of five other people. I read off the printed pages and didn't look up once during the entire fifteen minutes of the talk.

When I finished, I looked up from the pages that I held in front of me like a shield, and I was met with five faces of pure empathy and love. I still distinctly remember the look on everyone's face, and it still brings me to tears to think about it. (Literally, I am crying as I write this.)

Everyone gave me a hug and shared with me what was most impactful for them about my talk. They each shared that they could see parts of their own story in mine and thanked me for sharing.

A weight was lifted off of me that day. The empathetic, loving response I received reflected back to me that I am not the monster I was so scared of being—that was all in my head. That was my shame talking, and my shame was a liar.

The reason it was so impactful to have my truth, my experiences, and my story met with love and empathy is that it invalidated my own internal belief that I wasn't good enough to be loved and accepted by others.

The people in the room with me that day—some of them complete strangers to me—met my story with love and acceptance and proved my belief wrong. They reflected back to me that I *am* worthy of love and acceptance, just by being me. The parts of me I tried to hide from are the parts of me that make me the most human, and they're the parts others can connect with most deeply.

Because of this realization, I was finally able to set down burdens I had been carrying for half my life.

I was finally able to start talking about experiences that I had hidden from for half my life.

I was finally starting to wrestle free from the controlling grip of shame.

And it changed my whole life.

EXERCISE: GET REAL WITH YOUR SHAME

Part 1: Create Your Own Shame List

Part 1 of this exercise should be completed over the course of *at least* one week.

When connecting with my shame, I began by exploring my past experiences and I invite you to do the same.

Begin by thinking about the experiences in your life you often shy away from or hide from. If something comes to mind and you immediately think, *NOPE! NOT GOING THERE!* **write it down**.

If something comes to mind that causes any sort of physical sensation in your body (your stomach drops like you're going over the hill on a big roller coaster, your heart flutters or pounds like you just avoided a car accident), **write it down**.

If you're having trouble thinking of anything at all, I invite you to start with past experiences that you feel any sort of discomfort around. This could be a bad breakup, a mess-up at work, or just one of your not-so-finest moments. Write about the experience and ask yourself what about it feels uncomfortable to you.

I invite you to return to this exercise for at least five minutes (more is great!) every day for one week.

By the end of the process, you should have compiled a list of some of the past experiences you feel shame around.

_____

_____

_____

_____

Part 2: Sit with Your Shame

To the best of your ability, quiet your mind.

Next, bring to mind the first experience on your shame list. As you do, focus on the physical sensations in your body.

If you feel a sensation, focus on that part of your body and the feeling of the sensation. If the feeling intensifies, try to keep your focus and stay with it. You can repeat the words, "I am open to this feeling" out loud or in your head.

If at any point the sensation begins to feel too overwhelming, stop the exercise and move your body (go for a walk, do jumping jacks, have a dance party for one).

When this process feels complete, use the following pages to write about what came up for you. You can write about the past experience, your emotions, any actions you want to take—whatever comes up.

Repeat this process for each one of the past experiences on your list. Again, take your time. Focusing on one experience a day is a good rhythm.

_____

_____

_____

_____

_____

_____

_____

Part 3: Share Your Shame

The key to my experiences is that I shared in safe settings, with emotionally intelligent people I trusted.

I invite you to do the same.

Once Part 2 feels complete, share your list or your experience connecting with your shame with someone you trust.

A solid rule of thumb when choosing this person is to ask yourself, *Does this person have high emotional well-being and live a life I would want for myself?* If the answer is no, this is not the right person for you to share with at this time.

Sharing with someone else is a key part of this exercise, but the person you share with must be ready to receive your story. If someone has not yet faced their own shame, they will not be able to handle yours.

If no one is resonating with you to share your story with, that's okay. You may choose to turn to a therapist, if you're able.

CHAPTER 3

Become Aware of Your Thoughts

I HAD ALWAYS BEEN SKEPTICAL of meditation. Not of the practice itself, but of my ability to meditate.

I was under the impression that to meditate I needed to clear my mind of all thoughts, which rightfully seemed impossible.

I had tried meditation (and by meditation, I mean I tried to not think...*at all*) a couple of times because it seemed like one of those things you're supposed to do. After all, research shows meditation can have an array of positive side effects, including easing symptoms of anxiety, depression, and insomnia.[4]

But, despite the hype, I always felt frustrated and discouraged after my attempts to meditate.

As I began to acknowledge the behaviors I wanted to change, I realized these behaviors were directly connected to the thoughts swirling around in my head.

4　"Meditation: In Depth," National Center for Complementary and Integrative Health, US Department of Health and Human Services, accessed February 22, 2021, https://www.nccih.nih.gov/health/meditation-in-depth.

(Limiting thoughts equals limiting behaviors!)

In my quest to become more aware of my thoughts and how they influenced my behaviors, I decided to give meditation another shot. I downloaded an app to my phone that leads you through instructional videos and guided meditations. I started with "The Basics."

A gentleman with a warm, inviting voice slowly and articulately explained meditation and quickly crushed my notion of what it means to meditate.

Rather than clear your mind of all thoughts, the aim of meditation is simply to observe your thoughts, rather than engage with or react to them as you normally would.

Then, let the thoughts pass.

Just notice my thoughts? I can do that, I thought.

This seemed much more accessible to me.

With this newfound reassurance that I might not be "bad" at meditation, I started to meditate for ten to fifteen minutes each morning.

The process of beginning to observe my thoughts was shocking, to say the least.

I had no idea how often I got caught up and swept away in my thoughts. Even when consciously trying to observe and let my thoughts pass, I would get caught on the Train of Association.

On the Train of Association, one thought would trigger another and another and another, and suddenly I went from a calm mind to thinking about that school photo from fifth grade where I had cut my own bangs—and I would have no idea how I got there.

I would try to follow the breadcrumb trail of thoughts back to see how the Train of Association ended up at a distant stop in the middle of nowhere (bangs from fifth grade, for example). The thought trail was always random and the thoughts were loosely associated, at best.

When our mind is left unchecked, it goes on a trip, and until we are aware of the conscious, thinking mind—until we begin to intentionally separate from and observe our thoughts—we're just along for the ride.

Seeing how quickly and how far I could get carried away in my thoughts was eye-opening.

Beginning to understand I had the power of awareness to observe my thoughts, rather than get caught up in or react to them, was life changing.

For the first time in my life, I came to the understanding that I am not my thoughts. Previously, I believed everything my thoughts told me. As I'll talk about in the next chapter, my thoughts were often downright mean, and full of judgment and ridicule toward myself.

As I began to practice distance from and observation of my thoughts, I felt a sense of freedom from them for the first time ever.

I could more clearly see when my thoughts were based on judgment or fear, and I harnessed the power to stop my thoughts as they charged ahead on the Train of Association. I felt more in control of the stream of thoughts that trickled (or at times rushed) through my mind on a daily basis.

This is the power of observing your thoughts and is something everyone can learn to do.

Meditation is a buzzword for a reason. The practice of distancing yourself from your thoughts and stepping into the role of observer helps you build a relationship with your thoughts.

Once you have a relationship with your thoughts, you can better understand your thought patterns.

You can learn to not be consumed by your thoughts, but to coexist with them.

You can learn how to identify negative and fearful thoughts, then begin to work toward replacing them with more positive thoughts.

You can learn how to be more present in the moment, rather than ruminating about the past or worrying about the future.

Meditation is not about being in a blissed-out state of being, although you will likely find a sense of inner peace once you learn to not always engage with or react to your thoughts.

Meditation *is* about becoming more aware of your thoughts and building a relationship with them based on understanding and compassion.

Our thoughts help us make sense of the world and build our experience and our reality. Our thoughts influence our actions, behaviors, and sense of self.

We gain an understanding of ourselves when we observe our thoughts. We can work with our thoughts to build a reality that aligns with our goals and serves our greatest good.

The first step is to simply observe.

EXERCISE: OBSERVE YOUR THOUGHTS

I invite you to sit and observe your thoughts every day for one week. Start out small—just one minute—and add another minute each day.

Tips for observing your thoughts (aka meditation):

Choose a sensation to ground you into the present moment. This can be the feeling of the breath flowing in and out of your nostrils, feeling your belly rise and fall with each breath, or feeling your butt on your seat, or your feet on the ground.

The key to meditation is to simply begin again. Anytime you notice yourself swept away in thoughts, focus again on your grounding sensation and simply begin again.

In the moment when you catch yourself getting caught up in your thoughts, just begin again and notice what else comes up. Are you judging yourself? Do you feel frustrated? Notice what comes up, but don't react to it—observe, let go, and begin again.

The app I mentioned earlier is Ten Percent Happier (www.tenpercent.com). I highly recommend checking out The Basics course if you want to further explore meditation.

At the end of each day, take another minute and write down your observations.

DAY 1:

_____

_____

_____

_____

_____

_____

DAY 2:

_____

_____

_____

_____

_____

_____

DAY 3:

_____

_____

_____

_____

_____

DAY 4:

_____

_____

_____

_____

_____

DAY 5:

_____

_____

_____

_____

_____

DAY 6:

_____

_____

_____

_____

_____

DAY 7:

_____

_____

_____

_____

_____

_____

Bonus: Bring this practice into your everyday life! Throughout the day, can you pause and intentionally observe your thoughts?

CHAPTER 4

The Fear Spiral of Doom

AS I STARTED TO PAY more attention to my thoughts, I came to the realization that I was a bully to myself.

My thoughts about myself were rarely positive. The voice inside my head was judgmental and, at times, downright mean. I constantly put myself down.

I also realized that the voice in my head was a liar. Many of my thoughts were literally not based on reality.

Enter: The Fear Spiral of Doom.

The Fear Spiral of Doom is a close cousin to the Train of Association mentioned in the previous chapter, but in these cases, the train's destination is—you guessed it—inevitable doom.

Sounds dramatic, I know, but this is often where my fear-based thought spirals would lead me.

About a year after I started working at Scribe Media, I transitioned from a role coordinating work with our pool of freelancers into a role within the operations department of the company.

Around the same time, we made substantial changes to our creative process, and the new department leaders held a call with our freelancers to share the changes and news of my role transition.

I attended the call to listen, but didn't plan on speaking until one of the freelancers asked, "But what is Justine going to do now?"

The call facilitator invited me to share more about the work I would be doing in the operations department. Feeling unexpectedly put on the spot and not entirely comfortable speaking on a call with more than forty people, I explained my new role with a slight shake in my voice and a sense of uneasiness that I would get something wrong.

I honestly have no idea what I said, but I stumbled on some of my words at one point and that was that. The spiral started.

I'd stumbled on my words on a conference call and felt less confident than I would have liked. Not the end of the world, right?

WRONG.

As soon as I was done talking, The Fear Spiral of Doom kicked in and my internal narrative went something like this:

I sounded like an idiot.

I couldn't even clearly articulate the work I am going to be doing.

How am I supposed to actually do the work if I can't even clearly talk about it?

They must think I'm an idiot.

The freelancers must be happy they aren't working with me anymore.

My colleagues must be questioning my value here at the company.

They're going to see I'm an imposter and don't belong!

I'm going to get fired.

I will never find another job like this one.

I will be exposed as worthless to everyone I know.

I won't be able to pay my bills.

What will my family think?

They'll see that I'm worthless too.

I should just do everyone a favor and leave!

Maybe crawl under a rock of shame and hide.

No one will miss me!

I'll just die alone under my rock of shame.

That's what I deserve. Just me and my rock.

That would be fine.

I eventually landed in a dark, shameful place, which was actually a relief after the incessant worrying and fear of the spiral. During the spiral, I felt completely alone and afraid, which was even worse than the shameful doom at the end.

This is just one of many, *many* examples of The Fear Spiral of Doom playing out in my head. Spirals like this one happened to me all. the. time.

My fear-based, anxiety-ridden thought spirals weren't based in reality (the leap from *I stumbled over my words* to *I should go into hiding and die alone* is a bit of a stretch), but instead were rooted in worst-case scenarios—hypothetical and highly unlikely "what-ifs."

The thing is, although the hypotheticals were unlikely, my thoughts created limiting beliefs that rooted me in place, stunting my growth and ability to be my greatest, happiest self.

As this particular spiral demonstrates, I believed I wasn't good enough to keep a job I loved and that there was potential for me to be "exposed" as an imposter at work. This belief generally caused me to second-guess myself, shy away from putting my work and ideas in front of others, and assume everyone else knew more than I did, even in my specific areas of expertise.

I didn't feel worthy. My own fear of others seeing what I felt stopped me from performing at the level I was capable of. My beliefs and fear kept me from bringing my full self to the table. They kept me playing and acting small.

This can be true for almost any area of life: relationships, business ideas, passion projects, social interactions, financial goals, etc.

The Fear Spiral of Doom feels like being caught up in worrisome, fearful thoughts and haunting, hypothetical "what-if's," and the effects of the spiral seep into all areas of your life.

The what-if's might keep you stuck where you are, not able to take steps toward achieving your goals.

You might be deeply afraid to relish the good things in your life because you fear they will be taken from you.

You might constantly worry about how other people perceive you because your worth and sense of belonging is tied to what other people think.

You might feel like an imposter and worry that others will eventually figure out you don't belong.

The Fear Spiral of Doom is a real trap that many people fall into. Humans are wired to anticipate and prepare for worst-case scenarios. It's a survival mechanism—anticipate the danger before it comes. That's how our brains are programmed, even though in modern times our survival instincts can at times cause more harm than good.

Through meditation and the practice of observing my thoughts, I learned these spirals are not based on reality, and that I have the power to stop them.

But, the fear was real, and sweeping it under the rug and wishing it away didn't work. I needed to lean into, feel, and explore the feelings that were driving the fear spirals.

To feel safe leaning into fear, I had to learn to soothe myself in moments of inevitable doom.

Soothing myself did not come naturally to me. What naturally came up was anger and frustration that I had fallen into The Fear Spiral of Doom in the first place.

I had to teach myself how to both soothe and be soothed when I was wrapped up in feelings of fear, anger, and frustration.

This wasn't an easy task, but I found the quickest way to soothe these intense feelings was to connect with my younger self.

When I look at photos of my younger self, my heart swells with love and compassion. Soothing my younger self feels natural, so in moments of doom and gloom I've learned to see the fear and other intense emotions as that younger version of me. This practice allows me to both offer and receive love and compassion. It ultimately allows me to engage with my feelings in a way that is healthy and productive.

Soothing yourself is an important skill, whether it's to feel into the fear fueling a fear spiral, or to learn to lean into other heavy emotions or experiences.

Life can be heavy at times, and learning to soothe yourself through the moments of heaviness allows you to cope and build your resilience toward life's challenges.

EXERCISE:
WOULD YOU SPEAK LIKE THAT TO HER?

Part 1: Connect with Your Younger Self

Find a picture of yourself when you were younger; I recommend between three and seven years old. Through the photo, connect with that version of yourself. Use the space below to write your answers to these questions:

- *Who is this version of you?*

- *What does s/he dream about?*

- *What is s/he concerned about?*

- *Who does s/he look up to?*

- *What does s/he feel?*

_____

_____

_____

_____

_____

_____

_____

_____

Part 2: Speak to Yourself as You Would Speak to Your Younger Self

First, think about a recent experience when you were judgmental or critical of yourself. Using the space below, answer the following questions:

- *What sparked the judgment or criticism?*

- *What words did you use when speaking to yourself?*

- *What feelings did you generate from this judgment and criticism?*

Next, reframe this experience as though you're talking to the version of you in the photo. Continuing to use the space below, answer the following questions:

- *How would your feelings about the situation change?*

- *How would your words change?*

- *What feelings would you hope to elicit?*

Bonus Tip: I have photos of my younger self propped up all over my office. When I catch my inner dialogue becoming critical and judgmental, I look at these photos and ask, "Would I speak to her this way?" No, I would not.

I have found this to be a great way to short-circuit my own inner critic and replace those thoughts with more kindness and compassion.

_____

_____

_____

_____

_____

CHAPTER 5

Feel Your Feelings

ONE OF MY BREAKING points that brought me down the path of healing (and feeling) was the moment I realized intellectually understanding or acknowledging my feelings and *feeling my feelings* are two very different things.

Someone asked me recently, "How do I know the difference?"

The short answer: emotions happen in your body, not in your head.

When you're analyzing an emotion, seeking to understand what triggered it, how to control it, how to manage it, etc., you are *in your head* and *thinking*. You are not *feeling*.

When I realized fear was keeping me small and affecting my growth at work (and let's be real, in all areas of my life), I tried like hell to logically understand the fear with the hope that if I understood it, I could master it.

Years of therapy helped me to intellectually understand my past traumas and fears. Understanding helped me to be more self-aware, to recognize my deep-rooted fear of abandonment, what tended to trigger my fear, and how this affected my reactions and decisions.

I tried every which way to mentally jiujitsu the fear away, but the fear was still there.

One of the co-founders of Scribe Media, Tucker, always said things like, "feel your feelings" and "the only way out is through," meaning if you want to let go of an emotion, you need to feel it first.

"Feel your feelings" was not a concept that clicked with me.

At first, I almost subconsciously dismissed this notion. *I feel my feelings!* I thought. (lol, I did not.)

Or, *I don't have time to feel my feelings! I'm too busy!* (lol, also not true.)

Or, *There's too much to feel. I don't even know where to start.* (The closest to the truth.)

I prepared a long list of why feeling my feelings wasn't applicable to me, but the truth is I didn't know where to begin, or *how* to feel my feelings. *Not* feeling anything had become second nature to me, and I had no idea how to start feeling.

Step 1: Get out of your own way.

Trust me, I get it: feeling your feelings is not intuitive to a lot of us. I still have to be intentional about giving myself time and space to let emotions come up, rather than compartmentalizing, shoving down, numbing, etc., etc., etc.

But, we are our own biggest obstacle.

On a subconscious level, we've learned to compartmentalize, shove down, and numb our emotions because we hold too much guilt and fear around the feelings.

We instinctually repress and suppress emotions that feel too overwhelming. Repression happens unconsciously, out of our awareness, while suppression happens consciously.

Repression and suppression of emotions can begin in early childhood as a coping mechanism to help us feel safe when emotions feel too overwhelming.

Then, without being fully aware of the change, these acts of repression become second nature. Repression becomes our unconscious, knee-jerk reaction toward our emotions.

My initial reactions to the idea of "feeling my feelings" illustrated my orientation toward them. I was scared, confused, and overwhelmed at the prospect of feeling because I was so used to *not* feeling.

If you're disconnected from your emotions, the first step is to recognize that on some level, you're working against yourself feeling your feelings.

Your disconnection was a coping mechanism meant to help you feel safe. Honor the part of yourself that works to keep you safe, but also recognize you have the power to reconnect to your emotions and change your orientation toward them.

The first step is to explore your current orientation toward your "negative" emotions. I use negative in quotes because, in reality, these are just emotions, and we've placed a lens of positive or negative onto the experience.

Emotions are energy that move through your body, and **all** emotions serve the purpose to inform and motivate you. You *need* the full spectrum of emotions to receive all the information your body provides to you so you not only survive, but thrive.

From here on out, I will refer to negative emotions as heavy emotions. I believe this is a more accurate description of the experience of these emotions, which feel heavy, but also carry the weight of importance.

To explore your orientation toward heavy emotions, ask yourself the following questions:

- *What are your beliefs about heavy emotions?*

- *Do you immediately shut down when a heavy emotion comes up?*

- *Do you feel frustrated or inconvenienced when you experience a heavy emotion?*

- *Do you feel anger, resentment, or even rage toward heavy emotions?*

- *Do you run from (maybe even literally), shove down, or numb your feelings?*

If any of this rings true for you, this is great! You can now acknowledge your orientation toward your emotions, especially the heavy ones.

When you recognize your orientation toward your feelings, you can become more aware of when these knee-jerk reactions come up in your life.

With awareness, you can bring the intention to change into these moments of reaction.

I create a frantic feeling of busyness whenever I am avoiding a feeling I don't want to feel. I suddenly feel a ton of internal pressure around everything at work and work extra-long hours while still feeling behind. I tire myself out so I have no time for myself or my feelings.

As I became aware of this pattern, the sensation of busyness became a sign to me that there was something I needed to feel. In these moments, I am able to slow down and give myself time and space to just be. Eventually, with enough space, I can get to the feeling I am avoiding.

Before I can get to the feeling, I need to understand that my orientation is to avoid.

You must first recognize your orientation and the reactions that come from it before you can begin to change them.

Step 2: Give yourself permission to feel.

Like I said, feeling my feelings didn't click for me…until it did.

After all the intellectualizing of my fear, it was still with me, very much affecting how I showed up in the world and with the people around me.

When the concept of "feel your feelings" finally clicked, it was an "oh shit" moment. I realized I needed to *feel* my fear before I could let it go.

Oh, shit.

Tucker was right: the only way out is through. I needed to feel my feelings in order to work through and let go of them. No amount of intellectualizing can replace feeling.

My desire to be free from my fear (and all the anxiety, doubt, and insecurity that came along with it) overcame my mind's desire to stay safe. I gave myself permission and opted into my feelings, which is something I had never, ever consciously done before.

As soon as you opt in, you don't just magically start feeling your feelings, but it is a necessary step to commit to the path you're choosing to take.

Step 3: Go backward.

My fear was manifesting itself in my current reality, but the roots of that fear were in my childhood.

I didn't recognize the trauma I had experienced in my life until I started talk therapy and began to share my past experiences with others. I had this idea that people only experienced trauma in war, or if they were a victim of other violence or physical abuse.

These are certainly traumatic experiences, but trauma comes in all different forms.

A traumatic experience is one that affects your sense of safety and security, and typically leaves you feeling helpless, alone, and scared.

As Dr. Bessel van der Kolk shares in his book *The Body Keeps the Score,* trauma is a universal part of the human experience. His research has found that emotional abuse and neglect can be *just as devastating* as physical abuse.

This means a caregiver's emotional withdrawal, or regular childhood experiences where your needs were not met, can have a long-lasting negative impact that affects you into adulthood.

Especially as a child, any *feeling* of abandonment (whether or not the abandonment is real) feels like a threat to our safety and can be a traumatic experience.

Psychologists have observed that the *memory of trauma* is what continues to affect us long after the experience is over. Van der Kolk compares the memory of trauma to a splinter that causes an infection, stating, "It's the body's response to the foreign object that becomes the problem more than the object itself."

It's our body's reaction to trauma that creates issues that stay with us until the trauma is addressed and resolved.

Neuroscience research confirms the long-lasting effects of trauma. Brain-imaging studies have shown people with trauma tend to have an abnormally high amount of activity in the insula, which interprets information from the outside world and triggers our fight-or-flight instincts within the amygdala (the part of our brain responsible for perceived fear and threat).

For people with trauma, the signals from the insula to the amygdala are firing all the time, which can result in a feeling of constantly being on edge or imminent doom. These feelings are deeply ingrained within the mind and can't be soothed by reason or logic.[5]

So, for those of us with unhealed trauma, the emotional and instinctual response and the sense of not being safe continue to live within our minds and bodies.

When an emotion or belief is limiting us in the current moment, we need to go back to where that emotion or belief originated. This requires going back to some of our most painful memories and the emotions associated with these memories that we never allowed ourselves to feel. This work is best done along with a trusted medical professional to support and guide us.

Going back to past experiences can be incredibly challenging and also incredibly rewarding. This part can feel scary. Just know that you're going back to past experiences with your present-day awareness and emotional tools.

---

5 Bessel van der Kolk, MD, *The Body Keeps the Score: Brain, Mind, and Body in the Healing of Trauma* (New York: Penguin Books, 2015).

You have the capacity to heal your past self by feeling what you weren't able to at that point in time.

Step 4: Invite your emotions to stay.

This is a tough one, but trust me, accept all emotions that come up. Invite each and every emotion to stay forever.

FOREVER? You might gasp in shock.

Yes, invite all emotions, both heavy and light, to stay *forever*.

For better or for worse, no emotion will stay forever. The invitation helps you let go of your resistance to emotions. You will continue to run into resistance to feeling your feelings until you accept all your emotions.

When I started to allow myself to feel my heavy emotions, I would think:

It's okay. I can feel this so I can let it go...

Yep, feeling it, and then it will go away...

Okay, go away now!

No, really...I'm done. You can go!

UGGHHH! WHY ARE YOU STILL HERE? GO AWAYYYYYYY!

...and so on and so forth.

My openness to feeling the emotion was a great first step, but my goal of letting the emotion go was blocking me from fully feeling it. It ultimately made the process longer and more painful.

Anytime there is resistance against a moving force, the forward progress and motion of the force are slowed down.

Feeling with a focus on *not* feeling the emotion anymore is a form of resistance. You're not fully feeling the emotion.

Dr. David R. Hawkins describes the process of surrendering to our emotions in his book *Letting Go*. Hawkins states, "Letting go involves being aware of a feeling, letting it come up, staying with it, and letting it run its course without wanting to make it different or do anything about it."

Inviting emotions to stretch out their legs and stay is something I still intentionally practice when heavy emotions come up, but when I do this, and I *really* mean it, the process is much smoother.

As I've said, suffering is the resistance of pain. We cause our own suffering by resisting the emotions we don't want to feel.

The steps I've mentioned provide a basic structure to orient yourself toward your feelings, but only you can actually get out of your own way, opt in, go back to what you need to feel, and invite the feelings to stay.

GRAB BAG OF FEELINGS EXERCISES!

Feeling your feelings is the hinge of healing—it connects you to yourself in a whole new and expansive way. If my experience resonates with you at all, feeling your feelings can also be one of the more elusive and challenging parts of healing.

I encourage you to go slow and recognize *it's a process*. You aren't going to crack open your emotions overnight. Baby steps are the way to go.

Below are several exercises meant to help you connect with your emotions. I invite you to begin with the first exercise and focus on one exercise a week for the next five weeks.

I encourage you to continue to come back to these exercises as often or as many times as needed. These aren't one-and-done exercises, but are meant to be part of your ongoing healing process.

EXERCISE 1: GUIDED MEDITATION TO CONNECT WITH YOUR EMOTIONS

Listen to the guided meditation for connecting with your emotions: www. justineharrington.co/emotions-meditation.

Listen to the guided meditation every day for one week. After each meditation session, use the space below to write about your experience.

_____

_____

_____

_____

_____

_____

_____

_____

_____

_____

_____

EXERCISE 2: SPARK YOUR FEELINGS WITH A SONG

Every day for one week, listen to a song that brings up any sort of emotion for you. You can listen to the same song every day, or switch up your song choice.

As the song plays, pay attention to the physical sensations in your body. Use the space below to describe the sensations you feel without justifying or explaining them.

_____

_____

_____

_____

_____

_____

_____

_____

EXERCISE 3: FACE THE FEAR

What is your biggest fear?

Write this fear in the space below, then close your eyes and attempt to locate the fear in your body. Your fear could feel like a tightness or burning sensation, a lump in your throat, butterflies in your stomach, tightness in your chest, or something else entirely.

Write down your fear:

_____

_____

_____

_____

_____

_____

If you feel a physical sensation in your body, focus on the sensation and invite it to stay. I often say out loud, "I see you" or "I feel you" to acknowledge the emotion.

If you don't feel anything, that's fine! Your body is still providing you with information, so continue to pay attention and notice any other physical sensations.

Are you clenching any of your muscles? Do you feel any pain in your body? Are you breathing deeply, or is your breath shallow? Paying attention to your body's reaction to fear can help you recognize when fear is coming up for you in your life.

Once this process feels complete, use the space below to answer these questions:

- *Where in your body is the physical sensation located? (Your chest, your belly, your throat, etc.)*

- *What is the sensation you feel in your body? (Could be a tightness, tingling, pressure, etc.)*

- *When you acknowledged and invited the sensation to stay, what happened?*

- *If you noticed a physical reaction in your body (clenching, pain, etc.), at what other times have you noticed similar sensations? If nothing comes up now, I invite you to continue to pay attention and come back to document what comes up for you.*

Perform this exercise every other day throughout the week. Use the space provided to record your answers.

_____

_____

_____

_____

_____

_____

_____

_____

_____

End of the Week Question: Have your feelings changed or evolved since the first day you did this exercise?

_____

_____

_____

_____

_____

_____

_____

_____

_____

_____

_____

_____

_____

EXERCISE 4: CONNECT WITH PAST EMOTIONS

I invite you to go through a similar photo exercise as you did to connect with your younger self.

For this exercise, is there a particular experience or time in your past that you believe still affects you in some way? Perhaps the experience was one where you felt hurt, or maybe you hurt someone else. Perhaps you still feel regret, shame, or maybe confusion around the past experience. Choose something that you feel ready to work through and heal.

If so, find a photo of yourself from that time. Through the photo, connect with that version of yourself. (If you don't have a photo, that's fine. Just answer the questions below without it.)

Using the space below, answer the following questions:

- *Who is this version of you?*

- *What does s/he dream about?*

- *What is s/he concerned about?*

- *Who does s/he look up to?*

- *What does s/he feel?*

- *What does s/he desire most in life?*

As you write through your answers, pay attention to what's happening in your body. Make note of any emotions or physical reactions.

Remember to invite the emotions to stay as long as they don't feel too overwhelming. You can and should take breaks as you need to.

Once you feel the process is complete, I encourage you to move your body! Go for a walk, do some jumping jacks, or have a dance party for one.

EXERCISE 5: HEALING RELATIONSHIPS

If there's a relationship you'd like to heal, current or past, use the space below to write a letter to that person.

Write the letter with the intention that they will never see it and allow your true feelings to come through.

This is also a powerful exercise to do to heal your relationship with yourself. Is there a particular part of yourself or a past version of yourself that you want to heal your relationship with? If so, write a letter to that part or version of you.

_____

_____

_____

_____

_____

_____

_____

_____

_____

_____

_____

CHAPTER 6

Use Your Triggers to Connect with Your Emotions

HAVE YOU EVER BLOWN UP at a family member or friend for no apparent reason, and then regretted your behavior afterward?

Something much deeper than the surface-level situation or conflict was triggered, and you were reacting to that deeper emotion rather than the reality of the situation in front of you. An emotional trigger projects a past experience of a time you didn't feel safe or secure into the current moment.

Judgment is a good starting point to begin building self-awareness around emotional triggers and to practice diving below the reaction in order to understand the trigger.

Why judgment? For starters, I find self-judgment often arises in my meditation practice when I am already in the space to dive deeper into where the judgment is coming from.

Also, unlike the example of blowing up at a family member or friend, there are generally no other strong emotions at the surface when judgment arises, which makes the exploration process a bit more accessible.

Don't be fooled, though. There might not be other strong emotions at the surface when judgment arises, but there is a lot going on underneath the surface.

The first steps to change how you react to certain situations is to first identify when your reaction is rooted in a deeper emotion, and then explore the emotion your reaction is rooted in.

You can use the following steps to explore the roots of any sort of reaction or behavior pattern (angry outbursts, snarky comments, avoidance, the list goes on…), but I will continue using judgment as an example.

If I want to get rid of my judgmental thoughts toward myself and others, I need to first be able to identify when judgment happens, then seek to understand where the judgment is coming from within me.

Once I've identified a judgment, I ask myself the simple, yet powerful question, *Where is this judgment coming from?*

Then, I listen.

The voice I am searching for is not the chatty voice of my mind—the one I know all too well. I'm seeking my intuition. My inner knowing.

My friend and mentor, Jayme, says intuition is the very first answer that comes up, just before your chatty mind—your ego—kicks in.

If you find yourself debating the answer, or if you feel any sense of anxiety or uncertainty around the answer, this is your ego, not your intuition.

Your intuition is subtle, yet confident. Your intuition speaks once, where your ego speaks incessantly.

Listening to your intuition rather than your ego is a practice, like building muscle at the gym. You need to deliberately and diligently work toward listening to your intuition. It doesn't happen overnight, and it takes consistent practice and trust.

This is why getting into a meditative state for this process can be helpful. Sometimes, I have to ask multiple times, *Where is this judgment coming from?*

The roots of my own judgments are almost always planted in fear and insecurity.

When the answer comes up, I then focus inward on what I'm feeling in my body. Where is the emotion? What is the sensation? How big is it? For me, I often feel fear as a tightness in my chest, or a heaviness in my solar plexus, which is the stomach area.

Once I identify where the fear lives within my body, I speak directly to it and ask, "What are you afraid of?"

Then, I listen again.

My fear usually boils down to the same things, but it's still important to ask the question and listen to the answer.

I am afraid of not being enough. I am afraid of not being accepted. I am afraid of not being loved. I am afraid of betraying myself.

When the real answers surface, I continue to focus on the physical sensations in my body and I speak directly to the fear. I say out loud, "I see you, I feel you, and I love you."

This may feel strange to say. It's okay. Say it anyway. If you just can't bring yourself to say, "I love you" to your feeling, you may choose to say, "I accept you" or words that resonate with you. Say this as many times as you need to in order to really feel it.

Once I acknowledge and feel love toward that inner fear, the feeling typically begins to dissipate. As the fear dissipates, so does the driver of the judgment.

Over time, I've noticed compassion and love starting to take the place of judgment and fear. This takes time, but it will happen the more you practice acknowledging, feeling, and showing love to your emotions.

All emotions want the same thing: to be seen, understood, and accepted. Noticing your reactions—whether it's judgment or something else—offers you an entry point into whatever emotion your reaction is rooted in.

Once you identify the deeper emotion, you can then go through the process of seeing, feeling, and loving the emotion.

This is the path toward feeling your feelings and no longer being unconsciously ruled by them.

EXERCISE: YOUR TURN!

When was the last time you noticed a judgment, either of yourself or someone else?

Step 1: Once you have identified the judgment, quiet your mind and ask, *Where is this judgment coming from?*

Step 2: Identify what you're feeling in your body, where the sensation is, how big it is. Visualize the emotion and feel the sensation in your body.

Step 3: If you're feeling fear, ask, *What are you afraid of?*

If you're feeling something else, ask, *What are you trying to tell me? What do you need?*

Ask as many times as needed to receive the real answer from your intuition.

Remember, your intuition speaks once. Your ego speaks incessantly.

Step 4: When the real answers surface, continue to focus on the physical sensations in your body and speak directly to them. Say something along the lines of, "I see you, I feel you, and I love you."

You can adjust this phrase in whatever way resonates with you. The point is for the emotion to feel seen and accepted.

Once this process feels complete, use the space below to write down your experience and observations.

_____

_____

_____

_____

_____

_____

_____

_____

_____

_____

_____

_____

CHAPTER 7

Your Emotional Compass for Your Needs

I USED TO THINK BEING *emotional* was a weakness. I was taught that *being emotional* meant you were not in control. Not to be trusted.

So, I learned to be in control. I learned to hide my emotions from everyone, including myself.

When my mom moved out when I was fourteen, I shoved my feelings of loneliness and despair deep down inside and drowned them with alcohol for good measure.

When a grad school professor told me I wasn't good enough to be in their writing program, I up and moved out of New York City rather than facing the feelings of shame and unworthiness.

When I broke up with my now-husband, I threw myself into exploring "my walls" and past experiences to avoid the very real, very current pain of heartbreak.

When any relationship, whether romantic, friendship, or professional, veered too close to the potential of my feeling rejected, I left as quickly as I could without ever looking back.

Throughout most of my twenties, I stayed on the move, not giving myself time or space to feel anything other than the itch to move onto the next place.

Throughout most of my twenties, I also had little to no connection to what fulfilled me, what made me happy, and what I expected from the people in my life.

I didn't realize that emotions are a powerful compass for navigating the world and are necessary for identifying and validating my own needs.

Emotions are pieces of information that help answer some of life's most important questions:

- *What sparks joy within you?*

- *What do you need in order to feel fulfilled?*

- *What do you need to feel safe?*

- *What hurts you?*

- *What boundaries do you need to set with other people?*

- *What behavior is unacceptable to you?*

Emotions guide our personal sense of right and wrong, define our boundaries with others, and help pave our unique path toward living a fulfilling life.

By cutting myself off from my emotions, I also disassociated from my own needs. The side effects were less than desirable...

Because I didn't have an internal compass pointing toward my own happiness and fulfillment, I looked toward others to fill that void.

I learned to value everyone else over myself.

My happiness and overall sense of security were contingent on those around me.

I had no real identity of my own and was constantly anxious and on edge trying to people-please and morph into whoever I believed another person wanted me to be.

I generally expected less from others.

I had loose and at times nonexistent boundaries. This manifested most strongly in relationships, which meant I dedicated a lot of my time to making my partner happy without thinking about myself at all—until I swung hard in the opposite direction and pushed the other person away completely.

Part of the unconscious draw of being needless is that I believed the less I needed, the less likely the other person would be to leave me. I didn't realize that by not connecting with my needs, I built unhealthy relationships that were fueled by fear—the types of relationships that can never last.

The act of "being needless" was exhausting and, in the end, the only thoughts I had about myself were how I was perceived by others.

I only saw myself through the eyes of others. To myself, I was nothing.

I've talked a lot about how this manifested in my life: The Fear Spiral of Doom, judgmental and critical thoughts, etc., etc.

I was so wrapped up in my own thoughts (very different than needs!), particularly my thoughts around other people, that I didn't even realize I was neglecting my needs.

Hell, I might not have even realized I had needs above and beyond basic human ones, like food, water, and shelter.

If you have similar thoughts centered around what others think of you, your needs might also be taking a back seat. Or maybe they're not even in the car.

Maybe you're aware of your needs, but still put the needs of others first.

The process of becoming curious about myself, feeling into fear, and processing the emotions of past experiences brought me to a closer connection with myself, and what I need to feel safe, secure, peace, and love.

Through this process, I also realized that my past traumas were all experiences in which my needs were completely disregarded. Once I began to recognize my own needs and when in my past my needs had been violated or unfulfilled, I was able to better understand my own emotional triggers, communicate more effectively in my relationships, and hold healthy boundaries with others.

Here is one example of what this looks like in reality. My husband said he would be home at 6:30 p.m. for dinner and was late without letting me know. I was furious. My anger boiled inside of me with more intensity every minute past 6:30 p.m.

When he got home, my anger was full-blown boiling. Literally, my insides were hot. I didn't necessarily want to yell, but I definitely wanted him to know I was mad, so I stomped around and gave him dirty looks without saying a word.

When he asked what was wrong, I exploded with anger, and even though my plan was to *not* yell, I yelled something along the lines of, "YOU KNOW WHAT'S WRONG!"

We then promptly got into a disagreement that reached no useful resolution.

This exact scene would play out every time my husband was late. I didn't want to be angry at him, and deep down I knew I was irrational. But I couldn't keep the anger from boiling up inside of me.

Through understanding my own needs and identifying triggers from my past, I eventually identified the root of my anger. When he says he's going to be home and doesn't follow through on that, my fear of abandonment is triggered. I interpret his actions as saying, "You don't matter enough for me to be home when I say I will be."

Of course, this is not reality—his lateness has nothing to do with my worthiness and is not a reflection of his feelings—but emotions aren't based on logic and reason. Emotional triggers aren't based in reality. An emotional trigger projects a past experience of a time you didn't feel safe or secure into the current moment.

Once I realized *why* I felt so enraged, I was able to communicate this with him. This wasn't always the prettiest either. Instead of yelling, "YOU KNOW WHAT'S WRONG," I might have just replaced it with, "YOU'RE TRIGGERING MY FEAR OF ABANDONMENT," but offering him that awareness was the groundwork for more productive (and calm) conversations. Our conversations helped him to better understand my emotional needs and triggers and they helped me to feel seen and understood.

Connecting with your emotions and exploring past experiences where your needs were not met are both ways to recognize your needs.

Learning to recognize your own needs offers guidance on your sense of right and wrong, what brings you fulfillment, and it teaches you to look inside yourself for what makes you happy, rather than looking toward others for happiness.

The more deeply you understand your needs, the quicker you can understand your emotional triggers, and the clearer you can articulate your needs to loved ones.

Ultimately, the practice of connecting with, understanding, then honoring your needs is the foundation for true self-care.

To me, self-care *is* being in touch with your needs and honoring them on a daily basis. This can be as simple as going for a walk when your body is craving movement or taking a bath when your mind and body need to relax. As long as you give yourself what you need in the moment, you're showing yourself care.

Your needs are important for all these reasons, *and* they're important because you're worthy of your needs being met. But, before your needs can be met, you need to first get to know and understand them.

EXERCISE: YOUR NEEDS MATTER

The following questions will help you identify and connect with your needs. Use the space below each question to write your answers.

What are your needs now, in this moment?

_____

_____

_____

_____

_____

_____

_____

_____

_____

_____

_____

What are your needs from others?

_____

_____

_____

_____

_____

_____

_____

_____

_____

_____

_____

_____

_____

_____

What are your needs in life?

_____

_____

_____

_____

_____

_____

_____

_____

_____

_____

_____

_____

_____

_____

What would it look like to honor your needs on a daily basis?

_____

_____

_____

_____

_____

_____

_____

_____

_____

_____

_____

_____

_____

What is a past experience where your needs were disregarded?

_____

_____

_____

_____

_____

_____

_____

_____

_____

_____

_____

_____

_____

How does that experience affect you today? Are there any reactions still showing up in your life?

_____

_____

_____

_____

_____

_____

_____

_____

_____

_____

_____

_____

Think of a recent time when you reacted to someone in a way that felt out of control, or disproportionate to the situation. What needs of yours were disregarded or unfulfilled?

_____

_____

_____

_____

_____

_____

_____

_____

_____

_____

_____

CHAPTER 8

Understand and Fulfill Your Core Needs

DATA FROM STUDIES OF MAMMALS, from rats all the way to humans, suggest we are profoundly impacted by our social environment. We experience great pain when social bonds are broken, and the feeling of social pain is *just as real* as physical pain.[6]

We're wired for connection with others. The need for connection is so important that feelings of disconnect or loneliness can actually cause physical harm. A meta-analysis of seventy different studies found that social isolation and loneliness increases a person's odds of early death by 25 to 30 percent.[7]

The need to connect with others is a core need of being human. It's part of our survival instincts and is deeply ingrained in our DNA. Abraham Maslow, a psychologist best known for Maslow's hierarchy of needs, defined connection as "love and belongness."[8] Meaning, when we seek connection with others, we are seeking love and acceptance.

6   Gareth Cook, "Why We Are Wired to Connect," *Scientific American*, October 22, 2013, https://www.scientificamerican.com/article/why-we-are-wired-to-connect/.

7   Emily Nagoski and Amelia Nagoski, Burnout: The Secret to Unlocking the Stress Cycle (Ballantine Books, 2020).

8   Jessica Martino, Jennifer Pegg, and Elizabeth Pegg Frates, MD, "The Connection Prescription: Using the Power of Social Interactions and the Deep Desire for Connectedness to Empower Health and Wellness," *American Journal of Lifestyle Medicine* (SAGE Publications, October 7, 2015), https://www.ncbi.nlm.nih.gov/pmc/articles/PMC6125010/.

Many of the fears we hold deep within are fears around this core need not being met. We fear we won't be accepted and loved, and the pain of rejection hurts just as deeply as physical pain.

These fears manifest in our lives and affect our behavior in all sorts of ways.

Fear can cause you to push people away and end relationships.

Fear can cause you to procrastinate on that important project on your plate.

Fear can cause you to keep quiet when you have something to say.

Fear can push you toward anger and aggression with loved ones.

I could go on, but the point is fear is often intricately wrapped up in our most self-destructive behavior patterns.

Sometimes it can feel overwhelming to untangle the many ways our fear affects our behaviors. And that's fine; we don't have to untangle it all.

I've fallen into the trap of trying to understand *everything* about fear. Where did it come from? How has it served me? How has it affected me in the past? How is it currently showing up in my life? How can I release it?

I've spent many mornings feverishly scribbling in my journal, my pen unable to keep up with the flow of words pouring out as I desperately tried to understand my fear. I believed I *needed* to understand my fear in order to work through it. In reality, I just needed to feel the fear.

I would often leave these journaling sessions even more frustrated. My quest to intellectually understand my feelings would lead me in circles and to dead ends.

Emotions aren't based on reason and logic, and there's simply too much woven into the fabric of our being to dissect and investigate every single strand.

Eventually, I came to understand that as humans we all have the same core human need to feel accepted and loved. When we feel accepted, we feel loved. When we feel loved, we feel safe and secure in the world.

Acknowledging that our emotions—*especially* fear—are tied to the core needs that run through all of us has helped me circumvent the WHY!?!?!?! stage of trying to intellectually understand all the emotional complexities that come with being human.

There is value in seeking to understand our behaviors and emotions, but when it becomes the focal point, it's likely a defense mechanism keeping you from *feeling* the emotions associated with a belief or past experience.

If you find yourself stuck trying to untangle the knots of your emotions for too long, pause and remember: no matter where the knot came from, the core is the same and comes from a place of needing to feel accepted, loved, safe, and secure. Many of our thoughts and behaviors can be traced back to these needs.

For instance, have you ever said yes when you really wanted to say *hell no*?

Have you ever given up on your goals because you feared losing loved ones in your pursuit of growth and personal development?

Have you ever stayed in an unfulfilling or even toxic relationship or friendship because it felt comfortable?

Have you ever lied, or denied your own truth, in an attempt to fit in?

These all ring true for me.

These actions (or lack of action) are all examples of denying your own needs to feel accepted by others. This is where our need to look toward others for acceptance—a survival instinct from a young age—becomes harmful to ourselves and our desired growth.

As children, we *do* depend on others for survival. To be loved as a child means we are cared for and safe. As adults, we often still carry the belief with us that our safety and security depend on love from others. In reality, we now have the capacity to accept and love ourselves, which is the **only** source of love and acceptance that will make us feel whole.

When you aren't connected with your internal source of love and self-acceptance, feeling loved and accepted by others becomes more important than being true to yourself.

You do not need to continue looking toward others for love and acceptance. You only need to fully love and accept yourself.

Each and every one of us has a well of love inside of us, and you can tap into yours anytime.

You can give yourself the love you need and deserve.

You can show up in the world from a place of love rather than fear.

From this place of self-love, you'll practice true self-care, hold healthy boundaries with others, feel confident in your decisions, and ultimately act in a way that is aligned with your needs and truth.

When you finally come home to yourself and settle into the place of understanding you already have everything within to abundantly meet your own core needs...

This is the purpose of peeling back the layers and Going Within yourself.

This is waiting on the other side of your wounds.

This is the prize for ruthlessly seeking clarity around who you are from the surface all the way down to your core.

EXERCISE: CONNECTING WITH LOVE

I invite you to listen to this guided meditation to help you connect with the love you hold inside of you: www.justineharrington.co/love-meditation.

Come back to this meditation as often as you'd like.

CHAPTER 9

Connect with Your Magic

FOR MOST OF MY ADULT life, when someone asked me what I liked about myself, I would freeze. This question felt like a test that I'd likely fail.

I would panic and think, *If I don't come up with something convincing, they're going to think that I'm an awful person and they'll run away in fear!*

Yes, dramatic again, I know. But this was the internal narrative that played inside my head. I believed I needed to put on a performance for others in order for them to accept me.

I didn't accept myself, so I was constantly trying to be *somebody* for everyone else.

I didn't accept myself because I didn't know myself. I hid from myself out of fear of being exposed as somehow intrinsically flawed and bad.

So, when someone asked me what I liked about myself, I'd come up with something generic that sounded like the right answer.

I'm easygoing.

I'm caring.

I'm kind.

...

...

...

That was all I could muster up to like about myself.

I loosely believed these things about myself, but the fact is I cared only about what the other person thought of me. I didn't find my own opinion and beliefs to be valuable, even when it came to who I was as a person.

I didn't have an internal sense of worthiness, so I looked toward others to fill the hole where my worthiness should have lived. I was constantly reading other people to determine who I should be in any given moment.

My chameleon-like abilities to blend in served me in the moment, but ultimately left me as a shell of a person with no real depth or identity of my own. The act of blending in was exhausting and left me feeling empty.

A couple of weeks after I started working at Scribe Media, I flew to Austin, Texas, to attend my first company-wide Summit. At the time, the company had only ten full-time employees, who I would meet in person for the first time.

My stomach was knotted in nervousness the entire flight. When I got to my Airbnb, I sleepily crawled into bed only to lie awake tossing and turning until 3 a.m. My mind was reeling thinking about my coworkers I would meet the next day—and what they would think of me.

Not only was I exhausted the next morning, but the knot of nerves in my stomach was even tighter. I ignored my nervousness as I met all of my fellow coworkers in the flesh over breakfast tacos.

As I read the room, I felt completely out of my element. I was surrounded by extremely intelligent, passionate, self-aware people who seemed to know a hell of a lot more than me in just about every aspect of life (or so my mind was telling me).

This Summit was the first time I saw the Strengths & Obstacles exercise, and I was astounded at how direct, insightful, and caring everyone was toward each other. This was the first time I saw what it looked like to deliver hard truths from a place of love and compassion.

Everyone spoke the truth in a way that felt like a firm but caring hug. There was zero bullshit or pretending, which both intrigued and terrified me.

By the end of this Summit, I still wasn't convinced I fit in with my brilliant coworkers, but one thing I deeply understood was that in order to excel working at Scribe Media, I would have to push myself outside of my comfort zone.

For better or for worse, I was a master at ignoring my fear, so I pushed away the thoughts of not being good enough and dedicated myself to learning from the people around me.

As the company grew, I became surrounded by even more fiercely intelligent, caring, self-aware people. I grew to deeply admire and respect the people I worked alongside. I looked up to them (and often still believed I paled in comparison), and through these people I began to truly see myself.

I began to connect with my own strengths and recognize the things I liked about myself. Not just in a performative way to prove I was "good" to other people, but in a deeper, *this is who I am* kind of way.

This shift happened slowly over time and it didn't start within, but rather it happened *because* the people I worked alongside reflected back to me the parts of myself I couldn't—or wouldn't—see.

My zero-bullshit truth-telling coworkers celebrated me and my achievements. Loud and clear, they called out the strengths they saw in me. They said I was intelligent, trustworthy, thoughtful, courageous, resilient. And with care and compassion, they also explained the ways I was standing in my own way.

At first, I felt a deep sense of imposter syndrome.

Imposter syndrome "describes high-achieving individuals who, despite their objective successes, fail to internalize their accomplishments and have persistent self-doubt and fear of being exposed as a fraud or impostor."[9] I believed the people I worked alongside just didn't really know me yet. I felt I had somehow tricked them into thinking I was someone I wasn't.

But, over time I heard these truths reflected back to me again and again and, eventually, I began to believe them.

One of my coworkers and dear friend, Brittany, has been an integral part in helping me really see and connect with my inner magic—the true essence of who I am that lives deep beneath my negative self-talk and beliefs. The parts of myself that make me, *me*.

These parts were always there, but I couldn't see them because I was so caught up in trying to be someone else.

There have been many, *many* times when Brittany held up a mirror for me and showed me the true essence of who I am, *especially* when I was being hard on myself and refused to see my strengths and magic.

She's also held my hand as I worked through obstacles and challenges along the way.

Everyone needs a Brittany. Everyone deserves someone who will remind them of their true essence and hold their hand through the fire.

Connecting with your magic is an important part of the healing journey. It's through your magic that you'll find the power and motivation to shed light on the darkness and explore all of yourself.

---

9   Dena M. Bravata, MD, et al., "Prevalence, Predictors, and Treatment of Impostor Syndrome: a Systematic Review," *Journal of General Internal Medicine*, accessed February 23, 2021, https://www. ncbi.nlm.nih.gov/pmc/articles/PMC7174434/.

Part of being human is that we're conditioned to look at what's lacking, what *isn't* working, and where we can improve. This is why we're prone to negative self-talk and believing we are "less than" in many ways.

To change our thought patterns and beliefs, we must be intentional and consistently reinforce more positive ways of thinking. Change requires time, patience, and repetition, but it is wholly within our power to change the way we think and treat ourselves.

Often, we're not even fully aware of all the ways we put ourselves down and limit ourselves with our negative self-talk. My negative thoughts about myself were simply a part of who I was. I didn't even really notice them or recognize the limiting effects they had on me. I was just used to that way of being.

It wasn't until other people began blatantly pointing out my strengths that I realized I was completely disconnected from these parts of myself. It was through these people I admired and respected that I began to connect with my truth and my magic.

That was my first step toward loving myself. I surrounded myself with people I admired and respected and listened when they reflected truth back to me.

I couldn't see the magic in myself, but I learned to believe what others saw in me, and eventually that led to seeing myself more clearly.

THE BRITTANY EXERCISE

Part 1: Think of someone (or a group of people) who respects, admires, or loves you. This person should live a life you would want for yourself and have high emotional well-being.

Write down the words this person would use to describe you. If you're feeling stuck, ask the person to write down a list of words they'd use to describe you and send it to you.

_____

_____

_____

_____

_____

_____

_____

_____

_____

Part 2: Once you have your list, read each word, one at a time.

After each word, pay attention to what you're feeling in your body. Do you feel a tightness in your chest or stomach? A lightness? A tingling sensation?

Your body's response will help to pinpoint your orientation toward these attributes.

Are you accepting of them?

Are you afraid of them?

Are you doubtful of them?

There is no right or wrong answer, and I encourage you to let go of any judgment that comes up. Your emotional response is a starting point to dig into whether you truly believe these things about yourself.

Sit with the ones you're having a hard time accepting and give yourself time to fully feel into whatever emotions come up.

To help move toward accepting these parts of yourself, say out loud, "I am [FILL IN YOUR ATTRIBUTE]." (For example, "I am courageous. I am giving. I am resilient. I am loving.")

I encourage you to return to this list as often as you need to and repeat this exercise. See how your emotional responses evolve and work toward fully accepting all the magic you hold within.

The Going Within Process

CHAPTER 10

Going Within

I CREATED THE GOING WITHIN PROCESS from my own healing experience and journey. My journey was one of deeply getting to know myself so I could begin to heal the wounded parts of myself and love my whole self.

To create the process, I identified the key realizations I had throughout my journey of self-discovery and the layers of consciousness I dug into in order to reach these realizations. From there, I created a framework for others to embark on their own journey of self-discovery so they, too, can heal their wounds and discover their wholeness.

When I began my journey inward, my goal was to truly see and understand myself. I started externally by acknowledging my negative behavior and thought patterns that were harmful to myself and others.

I then sought to see and understand the me beneath my conscious thoughts and protective mind. The parts of myself that existed in my subconscious that I had not yet realized were present within me.

I made the decision to acknowledge the parts of myself I had been hiding from. I sought to understand my unconscious patterns, emotions, and ultimately my inner beliefs from a place of compassion rather than judgment.

I sought to recognize how these unconscious parts of myself were showing up in my life, and I chose to shine a light on the deep pockets of fear, shame, and pain I held within myself.

I sought to understand what parts of myself were no longer serving me, so I could then release them to make space to create new patterns and beliefs anchored in love, rather than fear.

I chose to question who I was as a person, which led me to uncover inner beliefs that were intricately and tightly woven into the fabric of my being that were keeping me stuck, confused, and scared.

We all have unconscious patterns, emotions, and beliefs. It's part of being human. It's so human, in fact, that many of us don't even think to question these parts of ourselves because it's simply who we are.

Here's the thing: you have the power to change who you are, but it requires you to do the uncomfortable work of questioning the parts of yourself that feel scary, overwhelming, or that you'd just rather leave in the dark.

When you intentionally bring the darkness of the unconscious into conscious light and awareness, you then have the power to change the parts that aren't serving you.

The process of bringing the unconscious to light can be challenging because these parts of ourselves are so deeply ingrained in who we are.

But, it is possible, and I will walk you through my exact process for Going Within and bringing the unconscious to light so you can begin to see, acknowledge, and understand all of yourself—*especially* the parts you've never thought to question before.

This is a process I continue to use regularly whenever I identify something I want to change. Whether it's changing a habit, behavior, or thought pattern, you can't change the surface level behavior until you unearth and tend to the belief that the behavior is rooted in.

This is why *within yourself* is where true and lasting change happens.

The Going Within Process is a framework for you to use on your own journey to more deeply understand the roots of your behavior so you can create real change for yourself.

This is a layered process. We will explore one layer at a time, beginning with the behavior you want to change. Each layer digs deeper into your thoughts, emotions, and beliefs that support and influence your behavior.

The intention of The Going Within Process is to uncover the core belief that drives the emotions, thoughts, and ultimately the behavior you're seeking to change.

The framework can be adjusted depending on your specific journey and needs. The most important thing is that you continue to ask questions until you get to the belief that is driving whatever it is you want to understand or change.

Awareness is the first step toward change, and Going Within is the practice of bringing awareness to the deeper parts of yourself—the You underneath your conscious thoughts and everyday awareness. The You that is really running the show.

The process I'm describing took me many months to work through. In reality, I am still working through parts of my own process because healing is not linear. I am always going back to previous layers with a new perspective and am able to glean a new level of understanding and compassion for myself.

As you get to the deeper layers, you can expect a lot of emotions to come up in relation to what you're working through. If you need to stop in a layer for weeks or even months, good. Take your time and remember why you decided to start this journey in the first place.

The tools and techniques I've shared with you in the previous section will continue to support you throughout your process of Going Within.

Through your work so far, you've learned to:

- *explore deeper parts of yourself you might not have thought to look at before*

- *observe your thoughts*

- *soothe yourself in moments of fear*

- *feel your feelings*

- *connect with underlying emotional drivers*

- *recognize and fulfill your needs*

- *acknowledge the unique magic that makes you, you!*

These are all tools that you'll need as you Go Within and continue to more deeply explore the thoughts, emotions, and beliefs associated with your behaviors.

The goal of The Going Within Process is to create deep and impactful change within yourself. This takes time, compassion, and patience. Use what you've already learned, seek outside support and guidance, take breaks, and trust the process.

The Going Within Process is a layered approach to uncover the deeper parts of yourself that influence how you show up in the world—your behaviors, actions, and reactions.

Your behaviors are intricately woven together with your thoughts, emotions, and beliefs. You can't change just one of these things in isolation. You need to explore all of them to see their connection and understand how they influence each other. You need to make changes at the deepest level in order to impact what's happening on the surface.

There are eight layers to explore in The Going Within Process, each with a theme and key question(s) to consider:

Layer 1: Behavior

Layer 2: Thoughts

Layer 3: Recognition of Emotion

Layer 4: Emotional Connection

Layer 5: Emotional Core

Layer 6: Safety

Layer 7: Belief

Layer 8: Root

The first layer is the behavior you're seeking to change, and with each layer we'll dig deeper to bring light to the unconscious parts of yourself that support and influence this behavior.

Remember, *within yourself* is where true and lasting change happens.

I know there's a temptation to skip ahead and dig right into the bottom layers, but a fast-tracked process doesn't work. (Trust me, I've tried!)

With each layer, you will glean a new level of understanding for yourself. With understanding comes compassion and the knowledge to create lasting and impactful change in the areas of your life where you feel stuck.

This process requires patience, openness, and a desire to change.

CHAPTER 11

The Layers

IN THIS CHAPTER, I'LL GUIDE you through each layer of The Going Within Process. I'll share what the process looked like for me as I peeled back my own layers to uncover the beliefs that kept me stuck in the same negative patterns.

I'll share my journey with you with the intention that it will show you a path you might not have seen before, or that you might see a glimmer of yourself in my story.

At the end of each layer, I'll provide you with key questions and additional prompts so you can explore and dig into each layer for yourself.

Just know, wherever your path leads you, you're not alone in your journey.

HOW TO APPROACH THE GOING WITHIN PROCESS

If you approach this process openly and honestly, with a genuine desire to understand, it will take time.

How much time is dependent on how deeply ingrained the belief is that you're working to uncover, but go as slow as you need to.

Slow is smooth, and smooth is fast.

The layers you will work through to uncover your beliefs are old ways of being. Meaning, they were likely formed in childhood, or at least at a younger age.

I invite you to view every behavior, thought, emotion, and belief you encounter as your child self. If it's difficult to connect with your child self, I invite you to view them as your own child, your pet, or any pure and innocent being you can connect with.

Would you judge or ridicule your child self? No, you'd likely feel compassion and empathy toward them.

Just like a child, the layers and beliefs you will uncover simply don't yet know any better, but you can be the compassionate teacher who shows them there is another way of being.

At each layer, you will gain awareness and see yourself in a new light. I invite you to pause and step away from the workbook for as long as you need so you can properly examine your realizations and connect with your emotions.

Take the time to absorb your realizations and be with yourself throughout. You've learned a number of techniques and exercises for connecting with yourself and your emotions, and I encourage you to continue to use these throughout your process of Going Within.

One last and important note: **expect the process to be frustrating at times**.

With each layer we become more aware of ourselves, but we don't yet have the full understanding needed to create real change. This can be incredibly frustrating.

You'll have an *aha* moment and think you have everything figured out, only to be even more painfully aware of how the thing you're looking to change is still showing up in your life.

This is not only normal, it's part of the process. The more awareness we gain, the more motivated we become to continue to understand so we can really, truly create the change we want for ourselves.

So, are you ready to Go Within?

LAYER 1: BEHAVIOR

The Going Within Process actually begins outside of us, when we identify something we want to change, such as a habit or behavior pattern.

I began my healing journey because I felt like I wasn't completely in control of myself, especially the habitual behavior patterns that were limiting me from growth and connection with others:

I obsessively worried about what other people thought of me. I could clearly see moments at work when I didn't speak up or didn't push a project through to completion. I generally felt anxious about how others perceived me. This meant I was ignoring my own needs and constantly sought external validation.

I had commitment issues. I had a pattern of pulling the plug and leaving the moment things became too *real*, I became too content, or I felt threatened in any way. This could be a relationship, a job, or a home. I either outright left without a second thought, or in some way self-sabotaged my way out of the situation (this is the more painful exit strategy, let me tell you).

I was masterful at the art of starting new over and over again, which at times served me well, and other times didn't serve me at all. Either way, I was eventually left feeling tired, alone, and uncertain.

I was emotionally closed off and guarded. I was so emotionally guarded that I didn't realize the huge walls I had built around my heart to keep others at a distance. I wasn't honest with myself about my emotions, and many of my relationships reflected my own lack of emotional depth.

With the guidance of supportive, emotionally mature friends and through talk therapy, I started to become aware of these patterns and behaviors. I recognized they were ultimately keeping me from my desired growth and the connection I wanted with others.

But, despite my awareness, the behaviors persisted.

Eventually, I hit my breaking points where my desire to change was greater than my desire to stay comfortable. I decided to get real with myself and dive deeper within, with the intention to truly understand the root of my behaviors so I could then change them and change myself.

EXERCISE LAYER 1: BEHAVIOR

KEY QUESTION: What behavior do I want to change?

DIG DEEPER

How is this behavior currently playing out in my life?

How is this behavior limiting or affecting me?

How is this behavior affecting others around me?

Why do I want to change this behavior?

How will I feel once I've changed this behavior?

How important to me is it that I change this behavior?

What is the behavior I am working toward?

*How will I feel once I've replaced my current behavior
with the new one I'm working toward?*

> *OPT-IN QUESTION: Am I willing to opt into some uncomfortable and potentially painful moments of realization in order to change this behavior?*

If you answered yes, explain why. Paint a specific picture of why this journey and process is important to you, how you currently feel, the changes you seek to create, and how you will feel once you've made the change you're working toward.

If at any point throughout the process you forget why you're doing this work, come back to this section and review your answers.

_____

_____

_____

_____

_____

_____

_____

_____

_____

_____

LAYER 2: THOUGHTS

Our thoughts are the surface of our minds. Our thoughts are always present and are therefore the most accessible layer of ourselves to begin to examine.

Once I identified the behaviors I wanted to change, I asked myself, *What thoughts are connected to or are contributing to these behaviors?*

Earlier in the workbook, I shared my experience of beginning to observe my thoughts. Meditation, journaling, and talk therapy (or talking with trusted, emotionally mature friends or family members) are all great ways to become more aware of the thoughts that influence your behavior.

The awareness of my thoughts helped me to realize how critical, judgmental, and downright mean I was to myself. I told myself everyone else knew more than me. I would put down my opinions, thoughts, and values before anyone else had a chance to.

I wouldn't have talked to others the way I talked to myself, so why was it okay to talk to myself that way?

My thoughts were laden with hypothetical *what ifs* that caused me stress and anxiety. (What if that person doesn't like me? What if I make a mistake? What if I fail? What if they think I'm stupid? What if I don't belong?)

These worrisome thoughts were such a part of *me* and my day-to-day life that I didn't even realize how they affected my actions and behaviors. I took these thoughts for truth without ever thinking to question where they came from or how they affected me.

Once I began to observe my thoughts, rather than just getting swept away by them, I realized the direct correlation between my limiting thoughts and my limiting behavior patterns.

I was constantly directly or indirectly telling myself I wasn't good enough, and my behavior patterns followed suit. I self-sabotaged and pushed away good people and opportunities. I kept other people at a distance so I could perform and be the person I thought I should be at any given moment. This felt safer than showing others the real me and risking rejection.

Once I recognized my limiting thoughts, I still didn't understand the driver of them, and I felt ashamed for having them. I practiced observing and not getting swept away in my thoughts, but the negative and limiting thoughts still persisted.

I had to dig deeper into the next layer and uncover the emotion driving my thoughts.

EXERCISE LAYER 2: THOUGHTS

Harness the skills you've learned to bring awareness to your thoughts. You can meditate on the questions below or simply start writing your answers.

I invite you to observe your thoughts without reacting and without judgment.

KEY QUESTION: What thoughts are influencing my behavior?

DIG DEEPER
How do I speak to myself? Is it with kindness? Judgment? Ridicule? Simply observe and try not to judge yourself or your thoughts.
How do my thoughts influence my behavior in general?
What are my thoughts around the behavior I want to change?
How do my thoughts influence the behavior I want to change?

_____

_____

_____

_____

_____

_____

_____

LAYER 3: RECOGNITION OF EMOTION

I call this the *why* layer.

Once I was clear on my limiting behaviors, and I began to recognize the thoughts that influenced them, I asked myself why these patterns were manifesting in my life. I journaled around these questions and brought my realizations with me to therapy to talk through.

Why do I treat myself more harshly than I treat others?

Why do I obsess over what other people think about me?

Why do I feel uncomfortable asserting my opinions, thoughts, and values?

Why am I afraid to truly enjoy the good things and people in my life?

Why do I keep myself from reaching my goals and potential?

The answers were ready and waiting. The simple act of asking *why*, with genuine curiosity and openness to the answer, is enough to uncover the deeper emotional driver behind your thoughts and behaviors.

When I answered my *why* questions, I had several realizations about my self-worth and confidence, but perhaps more striking was that I saw the same core theme throughout all of my answers.

FEAR.

My thoughts and behaviors were deeply rooted in fear.

Once I uncovered this layer, my fear seemed so obvious, but it was simply not something I consciously recognized before asking myself questions about my limiting thoughts and behaviors.

I'll say it again: the answers are ready and waiting for us. We simply need to be intentional and curious enough to uncover them.

I finally cracked the code! I thought.

I thought the awareness of my fear would give me the power to change it.

But I was wrong.

Becoming aware of my fear wasn't enough to overcome it. Instead, I just became painfully aware of when fear was holding me back, without being able to truly change anything.

Fear is a very common emotion, yet it's broad and generalized. I needed to dig even deeper to identify what I was actually scared of.

EXERCISE LAYER 3: RECOGNITION OF EMOTION

Ask yourself *why* for every thought and behavior pattern you want to change. The best approach for answering these questions is openness and genuine curiosity. Truly seek to understand yourself, without judgment.

KEY QUESTIONS:

Why do I [insert thought/behavior pattern]? (Repeat for each pattern!)

Once you've answered all your why questions, identify any emotion that repeats throughout your answers. This is the emotion driving your thoughts and behaviors.

What emotion is driving [insert thought/behavior pattern]?

DIG DEEPER

When did the pattern start?

....

Is the pattern constant, or is it triggered by certain situations?

....

What emotions do I feel before the pattern comes up?

....

What emotions do I feel after the pattern comes up?

....

How does this pattern serve me?

....

What results is this pattern trying to achieve?

....

LAYER 4: EMOTIONAL CONNECTION

Emotions don't exist in a vacuum. We all feel emotions in relation to *something*.

We have a fear of *something*.

We are angry about *something*.

We feel guilty about *something*.

We are insecure about *something*.

We are resentful about *something*.

Fear is a broad emotion. I had to dig deeper into my fear and ask myself, *What am I scared of?*

When I asked myself this question, the answer was again alarmingly obvious, but it was simply not in my conscious awareness before asking. (Do you see a pattern here yet?)

I was scared of being hurt. I was scared of feeling pain.

That makes sense, I thought. *Who wants to feel pain? Not me!*

Again, I stopped at this realization for a while, relishing the fact that I had a legitimate thing to be scared of.

But, still, this realization wasn't enough to keep my fear from being in the driver's seat of my life.

EXERCISE LAYER 4: EMOTIONAL CONNECTION

Seek to connect to the *something* you feel the emotion toward.

My behavior was based on fear, so I asked myself, *What am I afraid of?*

Ask yourself a version of that question that is specific to the emotion driving your behavior, i.e., What am I angry at? What do I feel guilty about? What do I feel resentment toward?

KEY QUESTION: What do I feel this emotion toward?

DIG DEEPER
When I think of this emotion, what is my immediate reaction?
Where does this emotion show up in my body?
What does this emotion feel like in my body?
What happens when I focus on the physical sensation within my body?
When do I feel this emotion most prominently?
Is there a specific situation or person that triggers this emotion?
Do I feel shame, guilt, or insecurity around this emotion?
How have I been keeping myself from fully feeling this emotion?

LAYER 5: EMOTIONAL CORE

We saw in the previous layer that we have emotions toward *something*, and in this layer we'll see that emotions are also driven by *something*.

I call the *something* that drives the emotion the emotional core.

The emotional core is a specific outcome we want to avoid, or it's an experience we want to protect ourselves from. This is what's driving the emotion.

My fear of pain caused me to act in some less than positive ways, but my behavior was actually meant to protect me from some outcome or experience I wanted to avoid.

To get to the emotional core, I needed to uncover the experience I was unconsciously protecting myself from.

I asked myself, *What type of pain am I trying to avoid? What experience of pain am I protecting myself from?*

These questions led me to the emotional core of my fear of pain.

I realized I was all too comfortable emotionally and mentally abusing myself, but I was scared of the unique pain that could only be inflicted by other people—the pain of feeling rejected.

And there it was. **I was avoiding the pain of rejection. I was unconsciously protecting myself from feeling abandoned by others.**

This was the first time I acknowledged the unconscious *something* that was driving my deeply ingrained fear.

EXERCISE LAYER 5: EMOTIONAL CORE

Whatever your emotion, it's serving a purpose. Get specific with what's driving your emotion by uncovering the outcome or experience you're trying to prevent from happening to you.

This is a key layer. You're getting to the emotional core of your behavior. Take your time here and use your tools to explore the questions below.

KEY QUESTIONS:

What potential outcome am I trying to avoid?

What experience am I protecting myself from?

DIG DEEPER

Is this a likely outcome?

....

How does my behavior limit the potential of this outcome or experience?

....

How has my protective behavior served me?

....

What other outcomes or experiences am I missing out on through avoidance?

....

How has this affected my relationship with myself?

....

How has this affected my relationship with others?

....

Is this something I've experienced in the past?

....

LAYER 6: SAFETY

Our behaviors, thoughts, and emotions are generally working to keep us feeling physically and psychologically safe.

To our mind, the familiar *feels* safe, even if the familiar is anxiety, fear, hypervigilance, or any other less than desirable emotion or state of being.

On a subconscious level we are programmed to re-create the patterns that feel familiar to us, even if these patterns have and continue to hurt and limit us.

As I became aware of the emotional core of the fear that influenced my thoughts and behaviors, I felt even more frustration when these thoughts and behaviors would continue to pop up in my day-to-day life.

I reached a point where I could reflect on my thoughts and behaviors in hindsight and clearly see they were rooted in fear of rejection, but I had little control over them in the moment.

I felt exasperated and stuck. "Why do I keep doing this to myself!?" I asked in frustration.

That's when a light bulb went off. I was afraid of being hurt, yet I was hurting myself.

I criticized and judged myself more than anyone else ever would. I self-sabotaged my way out of situations and relationships in a way that made me feel *less than*. I kept people at a distance. I opted out and knocked myself down a notch along the way before even opening myself up to the possibility of rejection.

I hurt myself before I gave anyone else the chance to hurt me.

I recognized my comfort in causing my own pain to some degree when exploring the emotional core of my fear, but at this moment, I realized the *why* behind this behavior: **I felt safe being the cause of my own pain**.

Self-inflicted pain was familiar and therefore welcome. Opening myself up to the potential of being hurt by others felt unpredictable and therefore threatening.

You can replace pain for anything that you're trying to control or that feels familiar to you, and the reason for creating this reality in your life is the same. The feeling of control and familiarity fosters a sense of safety within ourselves.

Even if the familiar causes us pain and suffering. We feel safe in that pain and suffering.

Seeing how and where you are re-creating familiar patterns, even when they don't serve you, is an important step toward changing these patterns.

You must also recognize that you're stuck in this cycle because it feels familiar, and therefore it feels psychologically safe. You need to recognize how your current patterns influence your sense of safety and security in order to re-create new patterns that also instill a sense of safety.

Disrupting your current patterns, even with the best of intentions, could feel very *unsafe* and needs to be approached with care and compassion.

The more you understand how your patterns contribute to your overall sense of safety, the more equipped you are to soothe yourself as you reconstruct new patterns that serve you. For me, my new patterns were to be kinder and more loving to myself and to open myself up to be vulnerable with others.

The latter felt terrifying and very *unsafe*, but with my awareness of how hurtful my current sense of safety was to me, I was able to soothe myself through this transition. I reminded myself that in reality, I *was* safe to be vulnerable with my loved ones, and even if being vulnerable felt scary, it opened up a whole new door to love I hadn't been able to access before.

EXERCISE LAYER 6: SAFETY

You've identified the emotional core of your thoughts and behavior, including what you've been protecting yourself from on a deep, unconscious level. With curiosity and compassion, ask yourself how this outcome or experience is already showing up in your life.

KEY QUESTIONS:

How is the outcome I'm avoiding already showing up in my life?

How do I contribute to creating this experience for myself?

DIG DEEPER

What patterns am I re-creating from familiarity?

....

What am I trying to control?

....

Do the patterns I'm re-creating elicit a specific feeling in my body?

....

When is the first time I remember feeling this emotion in my body?

....

At a core human level, what does safety mean to me?

....

When I think of what safety means to me, what physical sensations do I feel in my body?

....

LAYER 7: BELIEF

A belief is a thought that we repeatedly reaffirm to ourselves that we hold to be true. Our core beliefs are generally formed in childhood as a way to help us understand the world around us.[10]

The beliefs that are formed at a very early age are so deeply ingrained in us that we oftentimes don't consciously know we have these beliefs. They're just a part of who we are.

Our beliefs are the driving force behind our sense of safety, emotions, thoughts, and behaviors. This is why we must first explore and peel back the top layers in order to uncover our beliefs, especially if the belief is long held and deeply ingrained into your sense of self.

I understood I was deeply afraid of abandonment, and I recognized all the ways I was hurting myself in my attempt to control the possibility of feeling the pain of rejection.

To uncover the belief supporting the top layers, I had to ask myself what inside of me led me to believe I needed to fiercely protect myself from the pain of rejection.

The version of this question that you ask yourself will be specific to whatever outcome or experience you are protecting yourself from.

Approach this layer with deep curiosity and compassion and leave any judgment or resentment you might feel toward yourself at the door. You are delving deep into your subconscious, into parts of yourself that have been deeply ingrained within you.

Curiosity, compassion, courage, and empathy are so important in this layer because you might uncover something unexpected and maybe even toxic.

---

10 Rachel Eddins, EdM, LPC-S, CGP, "Uncover Your Core Beliefs so You Can Change Them, "Eddins Counseling Group, Houston, August 21, 2020, https://eddinscounseling.com/uncover-core-beliefs-can-change.

Peeling back this layer took time. It's hard to describe the full process in a way that represents the reality of how I uncovered this belief. It didn't happen with just one question or realization. It didn't happen in an instant.

Everything I had previously uncovered, and everything I continued to do for myself—journaling, therapy, meditation, reading, energy healing—all contributed to uncovering this deeply held belief. I saw glimpses of this belief many times before I actually acknowledged it and recognized how it affected my entire life.

As I peeled back this layer, I realized that I was terrified of being rejected and abandoned because I believed myself to be "bad" and unlovable. Deep down, I believed I deserved to be rejected and abandoned by others.

When I uncovered this belief, I felt a surge of intense emotions.

To acknowledge that I believed I deserved the opposite of what I wanted the most—to be loved and accepted—was like a punch to the gut. I felt confused and sad.

I felt deep grief and sorrow when I saw all the ways this belief had limited me and how it (maybe not so) subtly influenced me to keep myself small and afraid.

I also felt a sense of relief and happiness that everything now made sense. I more deeply understood the driving force behind all of the other layers I had worked through.

When I acknowledged this core belief, it was as if my whole life came into focus. A blurry photo became crystal clear, and the emotions, thoughts, and behaviors that had felt alarmingly outside of my control now made perfect sense.

This isn't the magic layer. Acknowledging your beliefs won't change them, but it is a necessary step on the road to change.

Prior to acknowledging my own beliefs, I felt like I was fighting a phantom ghost. I worked hard to change, but I was trying to hit an invisible target. Acknowledgment of your beliefs brings the phantom into reality so you can actually see what you're working to change.

EXERCISE LAYER 7: BELIEF

Everything you've uncovered so far is rooted in a belief.

Remember, a belief is a thought that we repeatedly reaffirm to ourselves that we hold to be true.

Our core beliefs are formed in childhood as a way to help us understand the world around us and can be ingrained deep in our subconscious, outside of our everyday awareness but influencing how we relate to ourselves, others, and the world.

Even if your beliefs are fundamentally flawed, painful, hurtful, or even toxic, surfacing them and accepting their role in your life is the necessary first step toward changing them.

KEY QUESTION: What inside of me leads me to believe I need to proactively prevent the outcome I'm trying to avoid? If nothing comes up immediately, take a guess at the answer.

Write out your answers to the key question until you uncover what feels like the truth to you. Make sure you write down the beliefs you uncover. Writing them down is an important step to acknowledging and accepting the beliefs that are alive inside of you.

DIG DEEPER

How does this belief make me feel? Write this down, or focus on the physical sensations in your body without feeling the need to name the emotion.

....

How is this belief tied into my sense of self?

....

How has this belief affected my feelings of worthiness?

....

How has this belief affected my feelings of wholeness?

....

How has this belief affected my sense of safety?

....

Is there any part of this belief I wish to keep?

....

How is this belief connected to the original behavior I wanted to change?

....

What new belief(s) would I like to replace this one?

....

Revisit your opt-in answer in the first layer, then answer this question: How does my new belief align with my original vision?

....

What is the first step to begin to change my current belief?

....

How will I know when I no longer hold this belief to be true?

....

LAYER 8: ROOT

Think of this as a bonus layer.

Gaining a general understanding of where a belief comes from is helpful, but it's also too easy to get stuck in the logic trap of trying to understand. There are pieces of a belief you might never fully understand, and that's okay.

Once I acknowledged the deeply ingrained, limiting belief that I was flawed and unlovable, the next question I asked myself was, *Where does this belief come from?*

As I sought the answer to this question, I worked with several other therapeutic modalities, including talk therapy with a licensed professional, energy work, writing about my past, and more.

I slowly uncovered that this core belief was formed in response to several traumatic experiences in my childhood. My mind spent a lifetime trying to protect me from these experiences and remembering and acknowledging these traumas was a layered process in itself.

Even when I got to a place of understanding the root of my belief, this understanding brought with it a new set of questions.

I am still working through the emotions associated with my past traumas, but I have already constructed a new, more loving and supportive set of beliefs to replace the toxic ones that were hurting me.

That's why I call this a bonus layer. This will be an ongoing process that doesn't need to feel anywhere close to complete in order for you to begin to change.

EXERCISE LAYER 8: ROOT

As I shared with my own journey, to answer this deep question you need time, patience, and most likely outside support and guidance.

Seek to understand to the extent that it's helpful, but do not wait on the answer to begin to change any part of your current beliefs that no longer serve you.

The belief you'll uncover grew out of a past experience—whether it's a specific event, or something you were repeatedly told throughout your life that you now continue to believe. If you choose to dive further into your past to uncover where your belief came from, I highly recommend you seek outside support and counsel.

Talk therapy, EMDR, brainspotting, and energy healing are all helpful therapeutic modalities that support this work.

I also recommend you find others who are on their own healing journey. There is no greater power than that of an empathetic witness to hear and see us as we heal our wounds and discover our power.

KEY QUESTION: Where does this belief come from?

THE JOURNEY CONTINUES

You are a different version of yourself than when you started this journey.

Throughout this workbook you've learned to explore deeper parts of yourself, observe your thoughts, soothe yourself, feel your feelings, identify emotional triggers, recognize your needs, and embrace your inner magic.

You've learned to approach yourself from a place of curiosity and compassion in order to more deeply understand your unconscious motivators.

If you've completed this workbook, you have connected with parts of yourself that were living in the shadows, and you now have the power of more deeply knowing yourself.

My intention is for you to feel a little more at home in your body. To live less in your head and more in your heart, where you can approach yourself and the world from a place of love.

As I mentioned at the beginning of the workbook, to heal yourself is to uncover a new way of being. The changes you make on the inside will be directly reflected in the world around you.

As we grow, life opens up for us. Dreams that once seemed impossible show up at our doorstep. This workbook is one example of how faraway aspirations can become reality.

As someone who deeply hid from my own truth, I couldn't have fathomed a reality in which I would share my deepest truths with others.

Yet, here we are.

As life opens up for us, our journey continues. We strive to seek our truth, which inevitably evolves along with us. We will face new and familiar obstacles along the way. Life will always be our best teacher, showing us exactly what we're ready to learn.

As long as we continue to seek truth and growth, the journey never ends, but the path evolves and changes along with us.

So, my friend, your journey is only beginning.

Through the work you've done here, you have grown and evolved. You have shed some of the old, outdated parts of yourself and have stepped into a new version of yourself. Just know there are many more future versions of you.

My hope is that you see the path in front of you and know this is *your* path. You have complete power over your journey and destination.

As you go, enjoy the scenery, take breaks, and pick up travel companions along the way.

The goal of healing ourselves is to be able to truly enjoy life. To connect with other people. To relish in the sweet spots and to surrender to the twists and turns of our journey.

There will be highs and lows. My wish for you is that you always know you have the safest space within yourself.

You are home.

ACKNOWLEDGMENTS

I WANT TO THANK MY husband, Timmy, who helped provide the safe space that allowed me to heal, then to share my story with others. Thank you for loving me, supporting me, and being by my side for the hugs, the tears, and everything in between.

This book wouldn't exist if it wasn't for my dear friend and soul sister, Brittany. Thank you for helping me see and embrace my magic and for planting the seed that I should share my story with others. As I said, everyone needs a Brittany, and I am so grateful for you.

Sending the biggest shout out and so much love to my Scribe Tribe, who showed me there was another way to live, helped me to take the first steps toward taking down my walls, and who continue to fully support me. I am still in awe that I get to work alongside such stellar humans, and I'm grateful for each and every one of you.

Speaking of the Scribe Tribe, THANK YOU to the Publishing Team, who helped me create the best possible book. My Publishing Manager, Ellie Cole, who has talked me off the ledge, guided me forward, and made the publishing process feel *easy*. My editors, Harlan Clifford and Paul Friar, who offered insightful and caring guidance on how to polish this book and make it shine. My cover designer, Anna Dorfman, who designed a cover that literally brought me to tears. And to Alexa Davis, who went above and beyond to help me dial in my message and create a stunning website.

A very special thank-you to my mentor, Jayme, who helped me not only face my fear, but taught me to take the b*tch to tea.

And to my magical friend, Alyssa, who has helped me heal on deeper levels than I knew possible. Thank you for sharing your light and for guiding me toward my own.

Finally, thank you to my friends and family who have been with me through it all. Coming home has been a sweeter journey with all of you by my side.

ADDITIONAL RESOURCES

ALTHOUGH I LEARNED A LOT from Going Within, I've also learned a great deal from others. Here are some of the most impactful books and online resources that have helped me to better understand myself, heal, and build a healthier way of being.

Books:

The Body Keeps the Score: Brain, Mind, and Body in the Healing of Trauma by Bessel van der Kolk

Burnout: The Secret to Unlocking the Stress Cycle by Amelia Nagoski and Emily Nagoski

In an Unspoken Voice: How the Body Releases Trauma and Restores Goodness by Peter A. Levine

Letting Go: The Pathway of Surrender by David R. Hawkins

One Last Talk: Why Your Truth Matters and How to Speak It by Philip McKernan

You Can Heal Your Life by Louise Hay

Online Resources:

Brainspotting Therapy, www.brainspotting.com/

EMDR Therapy, www.emdr.com/what-is-emdr/

The Holistic Psychologist, www.yourholisticpsychologist.com

Integrative Wellness Journeys, www.integrativewellnessjourneys.com

Made in the USA
Middletown, DE
11 May 2021